Beginning the Christian Life

6:30
10:15

Beginning the Christian Life

A Manual to Prepare the Young Believer
for Church Membership

Revised Edition

RUSSELL KRABILL

Illustrated by
Jan Gleysteen

HERALD PRESS
Scottdale, Pennsylvania
Waterloo, Ontario

The paper used in this publication is recycled and meets the minimum requirements of American National Standard for Information Sciences–Permanence of Paper for Printed Library Materials, ANSI Z39. 48-1984.

BEGINNING THE CHRISTIAN LIFE
Copyright © 1958, 1988 by Herald Press, Scottdale, Pa. 15683
    Published simultaneously in Canada by Herald Press,
    Waterloo, Ont. N2L 6H7. All rights reserved
International Standard Book Number: 0-8361-3458-3
Printed in the United States of America
Cover design by David Hiebert; photo from Anchor/Wallace

04 03 02 01 00 99 98   35 34 33 32 31 30 29
Over 75,000 copies in print

Contents

Learning About God

Jonah Learns About God

The first men and women who lived on the earth did not know as much about God as we do today. In Old Testament times persons were learning more and more about God. When Jesus came into the world, people learned the most about God. Jesus once said, "Anyone who has seen me has seen the Father" (John 14:9). Jesus himself was God. When people saw the love and purity of Jesus, they knew what God was like.

You know the story of Jonah. Jonah lived about 800 years before Jesus. In that day Jonah knew many things about God. Jonah was a prophet and told the people of Israel to obey God. One day God told Jonah to go to Nineveh, the capital of Assyria, to tell the people to repent of their sins. But the Ninevites were not Jews. So Jonah decided not to go because he thought that God did not love the Ninevites. In this Jonah was mistaken, for God loved them as much as God loved Jews.

To avoid going to Nineveh, Jonah ran in the opposite direction. He went to the seaport of Joppa and boarded a ship for faraway Tarshish. As soon as the ship put to sea, God sent a terrible storm. The sailors were frightened. They were sure that God sent the storm to punish someone on board. Finally they discovered the trouble was Jonah. He admitted his disobedience to God, and asked to be thrown into the sea. The moment he landed in the water he was swallowed by a great fish. There in the belly of the fish Jonah had time to think. He came to his senses and began to pray. At last God heard him and made the fish vomit Jonah upon the dry land.

Again God told Jonah to go to Nineveh. This time Jonah obeyed. The people of Nineveh heard his message. They believed and repented of their sins. When God saw their sorrow, God did not destroy their city. But Jonah had much more to learn about God's love. He was not glad to see the people turn to God. Read

7

chapter 4 of Jonah to see the difference between the attitudes of Jonah and of God toward the people of Nineveh.

Learning About God

1. *God in the First Verse of the Bible.* Genesis 1:1.

The Bible begins with the record of God's great work of creation. The Bible does not try to prove that there is a God, for there are evidences on every hand that God is. We do not try to prove there is a sun. We do not try to prove that there is an earth. Neither do we try to prove there is a God. The Bible is God's Word in which God tells us about himself.

Genesis 1:1 also suggests that God is eternal. God does not become old like we grow old. God was in the "beginning" before the world was made. God always lived.

We learn, too, that God is a God of power. God can act. God created the heaven and the earth. To "create" means to make. How did God do it? See Hebrews 11:3. The worlds were framed or created by the word of God. Notice the number of times the words "and God said" are found in Genesis 1. God's word was so powerful that each time God spoke something happened.

2. *God Is Father, Son, and Holy Spirit.* Matthew 28:19;
2 Corinthians 13:14.

How can God be three persons, Father, Son, and Holy Spirit, and yet be one God? People have tried to explain it in different ways. Someone has used the illustration of water. The same water can be ice, water, and steam. Or to put it another way, a man can be a father, husband, and brother at the same time. But it is impossible to explain the truth about God fully. God is too great to explain. We must accept this truth by faith. The Bible teaches us about God. We believe that God is a "trinity" (three in one) even though we cannot understand and explain it.

3. *God Takes Care of the World.* Matthew 6:26-30.

God not only made the world, but also cares for it and keeps it going. God regulates the sun, moon, and stars. God is in charge of the weather. God feeds all living creatures. People of the world sometimes speak of God's work as nature. They say that nature causes seeds to sprout and plants to grow. The Bible teaches that God does all these things. The Christian knows that God lovingly keeps and protects his children. This does not mean that sickness and accident will never come to a Christian. It does mean that if they happen, God allows them to happen for the Christian's good.

4. *Has Anyone Seen God?* John 1:18.
   a. What does the Bible say about God? John 4:24.
   b. How is a spirit different from a human being? Luke 24:37-40.

5. *Is God Alive?* Jeremiah 10:10.

Some people think that God is a great force, like gravity or electricity. In Genesis 6:5-7 we learn that God is a living person. What are some things God does? God speaks, thinks, plans, sees.

What does John 3:16 teach us about God? In 1 John 4:8 we are told that God not only loves, but that God is love. That is even more wonderful. Many people have a false idea about God. They think that God is like a monster in the sky who is angry with them. But this is altogether wrong.

God is a loving person. He is like the father in the story of the Prodigal Son (see Luke 15) who loved his son even when the son was disobedient. We understand God's love more fully since Jesus lived on earth. If we want to know how God loves us, we should study the life of Jesus. Read what Jesus said in John 14:9, 10. God was working through Jesus.

6. *How Great Is God?*
   a. How does God answer this question? Jeremiah 23:24.
   b. What did God tell Abraham? Genesis 17:1. He said, "I am the Almighty God."
   c. What did Jesus say? Matthew 19:26.
   d. How much does God know? Psalm 147:4; Matthew 10:29, 30; Psalm 139:23, 24.

7. *Does God Do Wrong?*
   a. God is holy. Isaiah 6:3.
   b. God is perfect. Matthew 5:48.
   c. God is righteous. Psalm 119:137.
   d. God is without sin. Deuteronomy 32:4.
   e. God always does the right thing. Genesis 18:24.

8. *Is It Possible to Know God?* Acts 17:23.
   Some persons say that it is impossible to know God. When Paul preached to the people at Athens, he told them that it *was* possible for them to know God. We can learn something about the greatness and power of God by studying nature. But it is only through the Bible that we learn about God's love and mercy. It is only in the revealed Word that we learn about God's plan of salvation.
   Because all people are sinners, they are strangers to God. It is only through faith in Jesus Christ that they are brought back again to fellowship with God. The way to learn to know God is through Jesus. See John 14:6.

Questions About God
   1. What is the difference between knowing God and knowing about God? James 2:19; Revelation 3:20.
   2. If God is love, how can God send the unsaved into everlasting punishment? 2 Peter 3:9; Matthew 11:28; John 5:40.
   3. In what way did Jesus help people understand God? John 14:9.
   4. Why are people afraid of God? Genesis 3:1-10.
   5. If God is everywhere, why have we never seen God? John 4:24; Luke 24:37-40.
   6. Does God work today? John 5:17.
   7. How do we know that God is a person?
   8. What is the difference between creating and inventing something?
   9. Is the Bible the only place we can learn about God?
   10. What is meant by "the Trinity"?

Reviewing the Lesson

Cross out the wrong ideas about God.

1. God has always lived.
2. God created the world but has nothing to do with it today.
3. God is a living person. God can think, feel, and love.
4. It is impossible to know God.
5. God is all-powerful.
6. God knows everything.
7. God is everywhere at the same time.
8. God has never sinned.
9. Jesus Christ is God.
10. The Holy Spirit is God.

Memory Verse

God is spirit, and his worshipers must worship in spirit and in truth. John 4:24.

Day by Day with Jesus

Jesus often visited in the home of Mary and Martha. Martha liked to cook big dinners. One day she worked very hard in the kitchen cooking a good meal for Jesus. She had no time to visit with him. While Martha cooked, Mary sat at Jesus' feet and listened to his words. She enjoyed listening to Jesus talking about spiritual things. But Martha grew unhappy because Mary did not help with the dinner. At last she complained and told Jesus to tell Mary to help. Then Jesus said something very important. He said, "Martha, Martha, you are worried about many things. Some things are more important than others. Mary has chosen the most important thing of all. She has chosen to have fellowship with Me and to listen to Me" (Luke 10:38-42, paraphrased).

Young Christians need to be careful lest they become so busy that they do not take time to spend with Jesus each day. All Christians must read the Bible and pray every day if they are to grow in their Christian lives.

11

Perry Pictures

Day by Day with Jesus
First Day. Review.

Review Lesson 1, especially *Learning About God from the Bible* and *Questions About God*. Do not stop until you are able to answer each question. Turn to the Bible references listed with each question to refresh your memory. Be sure to learn the *Memory Verse.*

Ask God to teach you the truth by his Holy Spirit. In your prayer thank God for saving your soul and for the blessings of the past day. Pray for the other members in the class, that they may continue faithful to Christ.

Second Day. Why Can't I See God?

Read John 4:19-24

I can't see God because God is a spirit. God does not have flesh and bones like I do. God cannot be seen with human eyes, but he has power. God can think, feel, and act. God can know and remember. God can reason and plan. God can feel joy and sorrow. God is not simply a force like the wind. God is alive. God knows and cares. God is love. God is a loving Father.

If you study the verses you just read you will find a certain word in every verse except verse 19. To know that God is a spirit is very important in worship. We cannot see God, but we know God is near; we can pray to God.

Third Day. Where Is God?

Read Psalm 139:1-12.

An atheist (one who believes there is no God) wrote, "God is nowhere," but his little daughter read it, "God is now here." The truth of this simple statement so affected him, that he was converted shortly thereafter.

Ask God to bless your minister and your church. Pray for the missionaries both at home and in lands across the sea. Thank God that he is everywhere. Thank God again for saving you from sin.

Fourth Day. Idol Worship Is Wrong.

Read Isaiah 44:9-20.

Something inside of people makes them want to worship. If they do not know about the true God, they often worship idols. Some West Africans worship a *fetish* which may be nothing more than a shaped stone, a bright bead, a stick, a parrot feather, a root, claw, seed, or bone. The fetish is prayed to and given offerings. If the prayers do not seem to be answered, the idol is coaxed and even told to do certain things. If the idol still does not do what the worshiper asks, it may be scolded, whipped, and even thrown away. This sounds strange to us. Isaiah taught how wrong it is for a person to make a wooden idol. Read verses 15-17.

Fifth Day. God Takes Care of the World.

Read Matthew 6:25-34.

Who feeds the birds? Who takes care of the flowers? Does God care for people? When God made the world, God did not wind it up as we do a toy, and then go away to let it run by itself.

God takes care of it all the time.

Finish these sentences by using your Bible. The New International Version (NIV) is used for the exercises in this book.

1. The Lord is good to _____. Psalm 145:9.

2. O Lord, you preserve both _____ and _____.

   Psalm 36:6. (To preserve means to save, keep, or guard.)

3. Who [God] gives _____ to every creature. Psalm 136:25.

4. If that is how _____ clothes the _____ of the field, which is here today, and tomorrow is thrown into the fire, how much more will he clothe _____, O you of little faith! Luke 12:28.

Sixth Day. God Never Changes.

Read Malachi 3:6; Hebrews 1:10-12.

People sometimes wish that God would change his mind about some things. We can be glad that God's will and Word never change. The Bible says that God's Word is forever settled in heaven. When God makes a promise, God keeps it. Sometimes people make promises and do not keep them. But when God promises, God is dependable and able to do it. Have you ever seen the motto, "Jesus Never Fails"? Do you think it is true?

Jesus Christ is the _____ yesterday and _____ and _____. Hebrews 13:8.

Seventh Day. Why Do We Love God?

Read 1 John 4:10-21.

We love because ___ _____ _____ ___. 1 John 4:19.

14

In our sin we do not love God. It is God who loves us. How do we know that God loves us? Take a look at Jesus. See him suffer on the cross. Watch him take the blame for the sins of others. Hear him pray for those who say evil things about him.

No one ever loved like Jesus. And to think he suffered all this because he loved us and wanted to save us! We want to return our love to him. We want him to know that we appreciate such love. We love him because he first loved us.

How much does God love us? The writer of the poem, "The Love of God," says that it is impossible to know how much God loves us. If the ocean were filled with ink and the whole sky were a piece of writing paper, it would drain the ocean dry and more than fill the sky, to write the love of God.

Thank God for sending Jesus to die for your sin. Have you ever told anyone else of the love of God? Why not tell someone? If you do, you will be a witness—something every Christian should be.

Working for Jesus

Tell your best friend about your new life in Christ. Tell this person that you have accepted Christ as your Savior and as your Lord. Jesus said that we are to be his witnesses. Each day this week tell a different person about your decision.

If you expect to grow in your Christian life you will need to do something for Christ. On page 140 is a list of projects you may do.

Learning About Sin

Peter Learns About Sin

Peter loved Jesus. He left his job as a fisherman to be with him. Peter, with his friends, James and John, seemed to be a little closer to Jesus than the other disciples. On special occasions, when Jesus wanted someone who would understand, he took Peter, James, and John with him. On the night before his death Jesus took these three friends with him to the Garden of Gethsemane.

Peter loved to be with Jesus, and Jesus loved to be with Peter. They enjoyed each other's company. But one day something happened which destroyed their fellowship. Peter sinned. It happened the night that Jesus was arrested. Peter wanted to do

right. He intended to be faithful. But he failed. He became frightened and followed Jesus afar off. He was afraid that he, too, might be arrested with Jesus.

When asked if he were a follower of Jesus, Peter denied and said, "I do not know the man." When questioned further, he not only continued to disown him, but he even cursed and swore. But Jesus was nearby; he knew what Peter had done. He was grieved. He turned and looked at Peter. Jesus' look of disappointment broke Peter's heart. Peter ran from the building, and cried bitterly. Peter sinned against his Lord. Their close fellowship was broken.

While Jesus was in the grave, Peter suffered alone. Those three days were long and dark for Peter. Would he have another chance to prove himself? He could not relive the past. If only he could again see Jesus and ask his forgiveness. But Jesus was dead.

After Jesus rose from the dead, one of the first persons he found was Peter. The Bible does not tell us what they said; neither Jesus nor Peter ever told. John tells us about one of their meetings. John 21. We can be sure that Jesus forgave Peter, from their conversation by the seaside. When Jesus said, "Follow me," there was nothing between Jesus and Peter.

Learning About Sin
1. *What Is Sin?* 1 John 3:4.

A simple definition of sin is "disobedience to the will of God." There are two main kinds of sins: sins of *doing* wrong and sins of *not doing* right. Both are disobedience. Take, for example, a boy in school. His teacher has a rule that no one shall whisper during study period. If the boy whispers, he is disobedient. He disobeys the rule. Now suppose the same teacher asks a girl to work some arithmetic problems, and she refuses to do so. She even refuses to try. She is not mischievous nor does she whisper. She does nothing. She simply sits. That girl is also disobedient. The Bible says that anyone who knows to do good and doesn't do it sins. (James 4:17). This includes not only actions but thoughts and attitudes as well.

2. *How Did Sin Enter into the World?* Genesis 3:6, 7.

When God finished creating the world, God saw that it was good. It was pure and happy. There was no sin. God made Adam and Eve with the power of choice. They could choose to love and to obey God or they could choose to disobey. God placed them in a beautiful garden. Here they were free to eat the fruit of all the trees except of the one in the middle of the garden.

One day Satan, in the form of a serpent, came to tempt Eve. He placed doubts in her mind concerning God's goodness. He told Eve that she would be wiser and happier if she ate of the forbidden fruit. Finally, she yielded and ate. She also persuaded Adam to eat. Adam and Eve disobeyed God. They sinned. Thus sin entered into the world, and sin has been here ever since.

3. *What Kind of Person Is the Devil?* John 8:44.

The devil is a person. He is a bad person. The devil is sometimes pictured as a man having horns, a tail, and carrying a fork. But the devil is a spirit, and no one has ever seen him. The name Satan, by which he is also called, means "enemy." He is an enemy of God and all that is good. He is our enemy and tries to make us disobey God. All through history he has tried to upset God's plan.

It was God's plan, for example, to send Jesus into the world to die on the cross so that we might be saved. How did Satan try to hinder this plan? Jesus was scarcely born until Satan tried to have him killed. Later Satan tempted Jesus to sin. He tried to persuade Jesus to save us by using another plan than God's. But Jesus won the victory over Satan.

Satan is still working in the world, turning people away from God. At the end of time, he will be cast into the lake of fire, where he can no longer work against God's program. Revelation 20:10.

4. *What Happens to People Who Sin?* Genesis 2:17.

God is the one who gives life. When people sin, they separate themselves from God. They are cut off from the lifegiver. They will finally die.

18

The Bible teaches that everyone is traveling one of two ways: the narrow way which leads to heaven, or the wide way which leads to hell. Heaven is a place of happiness and rest. Hell is a place of suffering and separation from God. After a person arrives at either place, one is there forever. In this life persons determine to which place they will go. To say "yes" to Jesus Christ, and to follow him, will lead one to heaven.

5. *Have All People Sinned?* Romans 3:10, 23.

Have you ever visited the slums of a large city? There are people in great need. Many are dirty, homeless, and friendless. Many drink and get into fights. Often the police come and take the troublemakers to jail.

Sometimes in the slum area there is a rescue mission trying to win persons to Christ and the church. We say, "These people surely need God. They need to be saved from their sins." This is true. But the Bible teaches us that all of us are sinners. There is none righteous, no, not one—all are lost without Christ: kings, presidents, millionaires, well-dressed, well-educated—all have sinned and come short of the glory of God.

6. *Is There Hope for the Sinner?* Luke 2:10, 11; John 3:16.

The whole story of the Bible is the story of hope. The word "gospel" means "good story" or "good news." When Jesus was born, the angel announced the good news. A Savior had come into the world. People were lost in sin. Now their sins could be forgiven. They could be saved. They no longer need be separated from God. This is the best news the world has ever heard, that believing in Jesus is the way to be saved.

Questions About Sin
1. What is sin? 1 John 3:4; 1 John 5:17; Romans 14:23; James 4:17.
2. What is the difference between temptation and sin?
3. How can one know what is right and what is wrong? Psalm 119:11; John 16:13.

19

4. How does Satan deceive people today?
5. Has anyone ever lived a perfect life? Isaiah 53:6; 1 Peter 2:22; 1 John 1:8, 10.
6. How can we get rid of sin? 1 John 1:7.

Reviewing the Lesson
Write the correct letter in the blank.

__ 1. The person who never sinned	A. Temptation
__ 2. Disobedience to God	B. Sin
__ 3. The author of sin	C. Has a soul
__ 4. God's goodness questioned	D. Peter
__ 5. The final result of sin	E. Satan
__ 6. How a person differs from animals	F. All
__ 7. The suggestion to sin	G. Selfishness
__ 8. A basic part of all sin	H. Death
__ 9. How many have sinned	I. Doubt
__10. He cried bitterly because of sin	J. Jesus Christ

Memory Verse
Everyone who sins breaks the law; in fact, sin is lawlessness. 1 John 3:4.

Day by Day with Jesus
First Day. What Is Sin?
Fill in the blanks. Use your Bible.

1. The _____ ____ _____ are sin. Proverbs 24:9.

2. Everything that does not come from _____ is sin. Romans 14:23.

3. Anyone, then, who _____ the _____ he ought

   to do and doesn't do it, _____. James 4:17.

4. Sin is _____. 1 John 3:4.

5. _____ _____ is sin. 1 John 5:17.
   The greatest sin of all is not believing in Christ. John 16:9.

Second Day. Adam and Eve Had a Good Start.

Read Genesis 1:26-31.

How are humans different from animals? What difference can you find in verses 24 and 26? Adam and Eve were made in God's image. What does that mean? It means that we are persons. God can think, feel, and make decisions. God made us so that we, too, can think, feel, and make decisions. God is also holy and without sin. That is the way God made Adam and Eve at the first.

When they sinned, they spoiled the perfect image in which they were created. Sinful persons no longer act like the holy God. Jesus Christ came to restore and bring back our godlike image. In this life the Christian grows more and more like Jesus. 2 Corinthians 3:18. But the complete change will not come until Jesus comes again. 1 John 3:2. Then we shall again be like him.

Ask Christ to take your spoiled life and to make it beautiful—like his. Ask him to take the hate and evil thoughts from your life and to fill it with good things.

Third Day. All This Happened Because Adam and Eve Sinned!

Read Genesis 3:1-24.

Fill in the correct Bible reference from Genesis 3.

1. The ground was cursed for Adam's sake. _____

2. The eyes of Adam and Eve were opened. _____

3. Adam was driven from the garden. _____

4. Adam and Eve clothed themselves with leaves. _____

5. God clothed them with skins._____

6. Adam and Eve were afraid of God. _____

7. The serpent was cursed._____

8. Eve's pain was increased. _____

9. Adam's body was to return to dust. _____

Fourth Day. A Bible List of Sins.

Read Galatians 5:19-21.

List the sins mentioned in this passage. Use a dictionary to learn the meaning of the words.

	Name of Sin	*Dictionary Meaning*
1.		
2.		
3.		
4.		
5.		
6.		
7.		
8.		
9.		
10.		
11.		
12.		
13.		
14.		
15		

Fifth Day. A Bible Photograph of a Sinful Person.

This is a picture of a sin-sick man. The Bible says that he is unsound from head to foot. Isaiah 1:6. Use your doctor book (Bible) to see what is wrong with the man. Write in the blank what is wrong with each part.

1. 1 Timothy 4:2	Conscience	____
2. 2 Corinthians 4:4	Mind	_____
3. Genesis 6:5	Thoughts	_____
4. Isaiah 1:5	Head	_____
5. Isaiah 29:18	Eyes	_____
6. Matthew 13:15	Ears	_____
7. Proverbs 15:28	Mouth	_____
8. Psalm 78:36	Tongue	_____
9. Isaiah 6:5	Lips	_____
10. Jeremiah 17:23	Neck	_____
11. Romans 3:13	Throat	_____
12. Romans 2:5	Heart	_____
13. Luke 11:39	Insides	_____
14. Micah 7:3	Hands	_____
15. Psalm 6:2	Bones	_____
16. Proverbs 6:18	Feet	_____

Sixth Day. The Person in the Gutter.

Read Proverbs 23:29-35.

Have you ever seen a drunk person? In the Scripture for today you see a picture of one. Persons such as the one in the story like to see the red wine in the cup. It looks good. They like the taste of it, too, especially when it is mixed with other strong drink. They spend long hours with their buddies enjoying the refreshing wine and having a good time. They drink until they are drunk. They jabber and babble all kinds of foolish things. They fall down and hurt themselves. They lie out in the weather or in the gutter all night. The next day they wake up very unhappy. They have a headache and their eyes are red. They are full of wounds and bruises. Their money is gone. Their families are hungry. The officers sometimes come and arrest them for the way they acted while they were drunk. They are miserable and unhappy, and all because of the sin of drink.

Drinking is like all other sin. It brings pleasure for a time, but it ends in misery. A Christian should have nothing to do with beverage alcohol. God saves us from the slavery of alcohol.

Seventh Day. Heaven and Hell.

Read Luke 16:19-31.

Some small boys were playing with an old trunk. One of them climbed in and the lid accidentally closed. He was locked inside. His mother tried in vain to open the lid. The key had been lost. The boy was still alive and was crying for help. But he was cut off from the life-giving air and would soon die if nothing were done.

Frantically his mother rushed into the street, screaming and waving her arms. The first car to come along was an oil truck. The driver stopped, found out what was wrong, then quickly went to his tool box and took out a drill. He rushed upstairs and drilled a hole in the trunk near the boy's head. Now the boy was able to get fresh air. He could live until the trunk lid was opened.

So it is with those who sin. They are doomed to die. Sin makes them a prisoner and separates them from God. Only Jesus can take the sin away and again give life.

Working for Jesus

Choose one of the projects listed in the appendix, page 140.

Learning About Jesus the Savior

Jesus Comes to the Rescue (Read Mark 5:1-15)

Jesus and his disciples were crossing the Sea of Galilee. As they neared the eastern shore, high up the bluff above the shore, they saw a graveyard. It was not well-kept nor beautiful. It was unlovely and gloomy, with many dark caves and tombs.

As the disciples landed, they heard a cry coming from the direction of the tombs. Suddenly, a terrible-looking man rushed toward them. At a glance it was clear the man was not himself. He was insane.

The Bible says that he had evil or unclean spirits living within. These evil spirits or demons made the poor man do strange things. They made him fierce and strong. They forced him to go naked. Because of this he had to live alone in the tombs. You see, it was really the power of Satan that made him act that way.

Once the people tried to tie him with chains and iron bands. But the evil spirit enabled him to break the bands and run back to the tombs. He was a pitiful sight. His body was covered with ugly sores because he continually cut himself with sharp stones. Night and day, he was in the mountains and in the tombs, crying and cutting himself. His friends were afraid of him. They could not help him, and he was unable to help himself.

Then Jesus came. When the man saw Jesus, he ran and worshiped him. He fell down at Jesus' feet and cried with a loud voice, "Jesus, thou Son of God. Please do not torment me." Then Jesus commanded the evil spirits to come out of the man.

The spirits asked to go into a large herd of pigs feeding on the nearby mountain, and Jesus allowed them to do so. Suddenly the pigs ran down into the sea and were drowned.

When the people of the community gathered to see this

great sight, they saw the demon-possessed man sitting at the feet of Jesus. They could hardly believe their eyes. He was no longer crying or cutting himself. He was wearing clothes and in his right mind. Jesus had done for him what no one else could do.

People today are still controlled by evil. They are filled with envy, lust, anger, and greed. They hate and kill one another. Sin makes parents spend their money for drink while families go hungry. Sin makes people act worse than wild animals. Many persons do not want to be that way; but they cannot help themselves. An inner, evil spirit drives them on. It is only when they allow Jesus to take over, that they can have victory over sin and Satan. Jesus alone can save them from their sins.

Cathedral Pictures

Learning About the Savior

1. *Why Do People Need a Savior?* Matthew 1:21.

The name "Jesus" means "Savior." All of us need a Savior because all of us have sinned and are, therefore, lost. Apart from Jesus, we are separated from God and it is impossible for us to save ourselves.

At the close of a service a stranger went to Dr. Stearns and said, "I don't like your preaching. I do not care for the cross. I think that instead of preaching the death of Christ on the cross, it would be far better to preach Jesus, the teacher and example."

"Would you then be willing to follow him if I preach Christ, the example?" replied Dr. Stearns.

"I would," was the reply.

"Then," said Dr. Stearns, "let us take the first step. He did no sin. Can you take this step?"

The stranger looked confused. "No," he said, "I do sin, and I acknowledge it."

"Well, then," said Dr. Stearns, "your first need of Christ is not as an example, but as a Savior."

2. *When Was the Savior First Promised?* Genesis 3:15.

The third chapter of Genesis tells the story of humans falling into sin. Immediately God promised a Savior. Someday a man (Jesus) would be born who would bruise the head of the serpent (Satan).

When Jesus died on the cross and arose from the dead, he triumphed over Satan. Remember, God sent the Savior because he loved us. See John 3:16.

Other promises in the Old Testament tell of the coming Savior. Here are a few:

a. He was to come through the descendants of Abraham. Genesis 18:18.

b. He was to be of the tribe of Judah. Genesis 49:10.

c. He was to be of the family of David. 2 Samuel 7:16, 17.

d. He was to be born in Bethlehem. Micah 5:2.

e. His name was to be Immanuel. Isaiah 7:14.

3. *What Does "The Word Became Flesh" Mean?* John 1:1, 14.

In these verses Jesus is called the *Word*. Before Jesus came to earth He was in heaven *with* God. He was not only *with* God; he *was* God. Jesus was God in heaven. He was God when he came to earth.

Jesus was also a man. The Word became *flesh*. He suffered hunger, Matthew 4:2; he was thirsty, John 4:7; he became tired, John 4:6.

He was both God and human at the same time. In this, Jesus was different from any other person who ever lived. Jesus was anxious for people to know him as the God-man. Once he asked his disciples, "Who do you say I am?" Most people in Bible times believed that Jesus was just a common man, but Peter replied, "You are the Christ." Everyone believed that Jesus was a man. There he was; they could hardly deny that. But they needed also to know he was the Son of God promised in the Old Testament.

When we are convinced that Jesus is God, it will make a difference in our lives. When Saul (Acts 9) realized that the man Jesus whose followers he was persecuting, was alive and speaking to him from heaven, he trembled and was astonished. Now, instead of working against Jesus, he asked, "Lord, what do you want me to do?"

We may not be able to understand or explain how Jesus could be both God and human. But we accept it by faith.

A certain man could not believe that the great and wonderful God would ever lower himself to become a man. One day as he went walking in the field he came to an ant hill. When the ants felt his shadow come between them and the sun they were frightened and ran in every direction.

The man who loved all living things and wished to harm none, thought, "I wonder how I could make those ants understand how I feel about them? They are perhaps afraid that I am some great monster and will crush them beneath my feet. How I would like to be able to help them to understand that I have nothing but compassion in my heart for every living creature."

As he stood there the thought came to him, "There is only

one way I could ever do that. If it were possible for me to become an ant I could tell them and make them understand." That is what Jesus did when he became human.

4. Why Was Jesus Called the "Lamb of God"? John 1:29.

Exodus 12 tells the story of the Passover lamb. This story helps to explain why Jesus was called the "Lamb of God."

The children of Israel were slaves in Egypt. But it was God's plan to free them and to lead them into the land of Canaan. One day Moses told Pharaoh that God said, "Let my people go." Pharaoh, however, refused to release the people. Then God sent many plagues upon Egypt. Still the king refused to give Israel their freedom. God had one more plague to send. He would pass through Egypt on a given night and kill the oldest person of each family in the land.

However, God had a plan to save the children of Israel from this terrible calamity. Each family was to kill a perfect lamb the evening before. God told them to take the blood of the lamb and splash it on the doorposts, both above and on the sides. They were then to stay indoors. That night when the destroyer passed through the land, he did not kill the firstborn of the families that had blood upon the doorposts.

The giving of life is important in God's salvation plan. In Leviticus 17:11 we are told, "The life of a creature is in the blood . . . it is the blood that makes atonement for one's life." The Hebrew word "atonement" means "to cover." The soul of a person is separated from God because of sin. The blood covers or takes away the sin, and brings a person and God together again.

It is really the blood of Christ that cleanses us from sin. The sacrificial lambs killed in Old Testament times pointed forward to the lamb of God who would one day give his life's blood for the sins of the world.

5. How Was Jesus Our Substitute? Isaiah 53:6; Hebrews 2:9.

In a ball game when one player replaces another we call that person a "substitute." The word "substitute" is not found in the

Bible, but the idea is there. Because all sinned, all deserve to die. But Jesus died in our place. He became our substitute. He tasted death for everyone. Hebrews 2:9.

The night of Jesus' trial, Pilate suggested that Jesus be set free. Neither he nor Herod could find anything wrong with Jesus. Every year, at the feast of the Passover, it was Pilate's custom to release one of the prisoners. He therefore suggested to the Jews that Jesus be released. He thought that if he gave them a choice between Jesus and wicked Barabbas, they would choose Jesus. But Pilate was mistaken. Instead of choosing Jesus, they chose Barabbas. The result was that the sinless Jesus died.

6. *Is Jesus Able to Save Us from Our Sins?* Matthew 9:1-8.

How did Jesus prove his power to forgive sin? Jesus by his life proved his power over sin and Satan.

    a. He refused to yield to temptation. Matthew 4:1-11.

    b. The devils obeyed him. Matthew 8:31.

    c. Death, the result of sin, could not hold him in the grave. Matthew 28:5, 6.

In 1 Corinthians 1:24 Paul calls Christ "the power of God." If Jesus is God, then he can do anything God can do; and God is all-powerful. What did Jesus say in Matthew 28:18?

Questions About the Savior from Sin

1. What did it cost Jesus to come to earth? Philippians 2:5-8.
2. Why did God wait so long to send the Savior after the fall in the Garden of Eden? Galatians 4:4.
3. To be saved, must we believe that Jesus is more than a good example? Luke 23:4; Matthew 27:24-26.
4. Could anyone else, besides Jesus, have been the Savior?
5. Why was Jesus willing to give his life on the cross? Hebrews 12:2; John 13:1.
6. What was the main reason that Jesus came to earth? Luke 19:10; Matthew 20:28.
7. Is it possible to learn about God by studying the life of Jesus? John 14:7-11.

Reviewing the Lesson
Put (x) in front of each sentence which describes Jesus.
— 1. He was a sinner before his baptism.
— 2. He became acquainted with God at the age of twelve.
— 3. He was the Savior promised in Genesis 3:15.
— 4. He came to earth mainly to show us how to live.
— 5. He has power to forgive sins.
— 6. He has power to change lives.
— 7. He was both God and man at the same time.
— 8. His blood washes away sin.
— 9. He died on the cross in our place.
—10. He is the only one who can save us from our sins.
—11. He has more power than Satan.
—12. He had to die on the cross in order to be the Savior.

Just as Moses lifted up the snake in the desert, so the Son of Man must be lifted up, that everyone who believes in him may have eternal life. For God so loved the world that he gave his one and only Son, that whoever believes in him shall not perish but have eternal life. John 3:14-16.

If you read Numbers 21:6-9 you will better understand the memory verses.

Remember the Death of Jesus (1 Corinthians 11:23-26)
Our church has communion services, celebrating the Lord's Supper, at least twice a year. Communion is sometimes called an ordinance, an outward act which teaches an inner meaning. An ordinance uses physical things to remind us of spiritual truth. In communion, for example, bread and grape juice are used; in baptism, water; in anointing, oil; and in foot washing, water.

This is a good time to think about communion. We just mentioned the Passover Lamb. Each year the Jews observed the Passover Feast in memory of their deliverance from Egypt. The night of Jesus' betrayal, he and his disciples were observing this feast. Toward the end of the feast, however, Jesus began a new ordinance which his followers were to practice. This was to help

31

them remember his suffering and death to save them from sin and death.

Thus communion reminds Christians that Jesus died on the cross for them, as their substitute. The bread stands for his body, which was nailed and pierced. The cup stands for his blood that was shed to wash away sin.

Jesus was wise in giving his followers this practice. Not only does it keep before them his suffering and death, but also it speaks of unity of believers and is a source of spiritual strength and blessing.

Before taking part in communion, believers are told to examine themselves to be sure they are living the way they ought. They must confess and repent of sin, so that they are at peace with God. They must be sure there is no ill will in their hearts toward other people. They must be sure that they are in harmony with the church as it attempts to apply in a practical way the principles of God's Word to everyday living.

Only those who have examined themselves, and who have the same faithful commitment to Christ, should fellowship together in the communion.

A Living Bridge

Agassiz, the great scientist, as a boy, was skating one day with his little brother. They were gliding along together a little way from the shore. Suddenly, they came to a great crack in the ice. As the older brother, Agassiz was strong, so he simply jumped over the crack. Looking back, he saw his little brother standing on the edge; he was not big enough to jump across. So Agassiz came back, kneeled down, reached over the chasm, put his hands on the ice on the other side and let his little brother use his back as a bridge. Jesus did much the same for us.

Day by Day with Jesus
First Day. God's Long-Range Plan.

Read Mark 12:1-12.

The householder is God, who treated his people with tender love. God planted his people, the Jews, in the land of promise and protected them. God supplied all their needs. Afterward, God sent his servants to see how they were getting along and to receive of the fruit. The wicked people mistreated the servants, beating

33

some and killing others. At last God sent his Son. But they killed the Son and threw him out of the vineyard.

From the beginning God has loved his people and has tried to win their love. After Adam and Eve sinned, God promised a Savior from sin. From the beginning God planned to save mankind. God did not suddenly decide to send Jesus into the world. How long ago did God choose us for himself?

Read Ephesians 1:4 and fill in the missing words.

For he _____ us in him _____ the _____

of the _____ to be _____ and _____ in his sight.

Thank God for loving you before you were born.

Second Day. The Shedding of Blood.

Read Leviticus 4:27-31; 17:11.

The word "blood" is used hundreds of times in the Bible. From cover to cover the Bible refers to blood which stands for life. Life is in the blood.

When Adam sinned, it meant death for him. The only way he could escape was if someone else would die in his place. Someone had to die. Blood had to be shed. God may have been trying to teach Adam this truth when he clothed him with skins in the Garden of Eden. To get the skins, animals had to be killed. Innocent animals were killed instead of the guilty people. Genesis 3:21 teaches three things:

1. Salvation must be of the Lord.
2. It must be by the death of an innocent substitute.
3. Blood must be shed.

All through the Old Testament God taught that people must kill animals as a sacrifice for sins. But of course the blood of an animal could never take away the sin. The Old Testament sacrifices only pointed forward to the death of Jesus on the cross. An innocent person had to die for all of us who are guilty.

Thank Jesus for giving his blood for your salvation. Ask him to lead always in his way instead of your own.

Third Day. Jesus Is in the Whole Bible.
Read Luke 24:25-27.

The entire Bible tells about Jesus. The Old Testament points forward to him and the New Testament points backward.

OLD TESTAMENT ⇨ *Christ* ⇦ NEW TESTAMENT

Christ is the key that unlocks the meaning of the Bible. It is not until we understand the saving work on Jesus on earth that we can know the full meaning of the sacrifices, the tabernacle, and the ceremonies of the Old Testament. The death of Jesus on the cross, for example, helps to explain the meaning of the snake on the pole. See Numbers 21:6-9 and John 3:14-16.

A little boy was asked to put a difficult puzzle together. He did so in a very short time, much to the surprise of his friends. "How did you do it so quickly?" they asked. "There was a picture of a man's face on the back," he replied. The Bible also is a hard puzzle to put together until we look for the face of Jesus in it.

Ask God to help you understand the Bible.

Fourth Day. The Love of God.
Read 1 John 4:8-11; John 3:16.

We are sure that God loves us because he gave his only Son to die for us. He wasn't forced to do it. God did it because he loved us. Peter Mackenzie, a Methodist minister, preached a sermon on John 3:16. He began by saying, "When God loves, he loves a world. When he gives, he gives his Son.

"Fond parents often say to a little child: 'How much do you love me?' The answer is usually a kiss and a hug. If you put the same question to our heavenly Father, the answer is—the cross. . . . We can glimpse the sufferings of Christ in the Garden and on Calvary; but who can picture the sorrows of the Father in heaven in that last hour?"—*The Boston Transcript.*

Thank God for loving you even when you were a sinner.

Fifth Day. *Jesus Died for All People.*

Read John 3:16; 1 John 2:2.
Use your Bible to fill in the missing words.

1. Romans 1:16. I am not ashamed _____ _____ _____. because it is the _____ ____ _____ for the salvation of _____ who believes.

2. Romans 5:6. You see, at just the _____ _____, when we were still _____, Christ died for the _____.

3. Romans 5:7,8. Very _____ will anyone _____ for a righteous man, though for a good man someone might _____ dare to die. But God demonstrates his own love _____ ____ in this: While we were still _____, Christ _____ for us.

A dozen shipwrecked persons were in an overloaded boat. To lighten the load one of them jumped overboard and the rest were saved. For which of the eleven did the sailor give up life? If Christ died for all, he died for each of us; for no one more than another; no one is omitted. The sun shines on millions of people each day. But I know that it shines for me, and would shine tomorrow morning if not another soul were left on the earth. So Christ loved me and gave himself for me.

Thank the Lord Jesus for dying for you.

Sixth Day. *Some Words to Learn.*

Use your Bible and dictionary to learn the meanings of the following words.

1. Sacrifice. Hebrews 10:12 (Dictionary meaning) _____

2. Ransom. Matthew 20:28 _____

_____

3. Atonement. Hebrews 2:17_____

_____

The Bible cannot explain what Jesus did for us with only one word. It takes many words to describe the work of Jesus. Each word shows us another side or angle of the truth. Several blind men went to "see" an elephant. One man felt the elephant's leg and thought the elephant was like a tree. Another felt his tail and thought the elephant was like a rope. Still another felt the elephant's side and thought he was like a wall. In a sense they were all right, but the complete picture was a combination of all the descriptions.

Seventh Day. One Way to Heaven.
Read John 14:6; Acts 4:10-12.

Jesus is not *a* way to heaven; He is *the* way. People sometimes say, "You get to heaven your way and I'll get to heaven my way," as if to get to heaven we invent our own way. There is only *one* way to heaven. That way is Jesus Christ.

Look up these references and fill in the blanks.

1. Proverbs 14:12. Our own way leads to _____

2. Matthew 7:14. God's narrow way leads to_____

Ask Jesus to keep you on the right way.

Working for Jesus
How are you getting along with your projects? The Christian life is a life of service. A minister said, "If my members do not become active in the work of the church as soon as they accept Christ I begin to wonder whether they are saved." Work on suggestions 8, 9, and 10 on page 140.

Lesson 4

Accepting the Savior

How a Tax Collector Received Christ

Zacchaeus was a rich man. But he was not happy. Zacchaeus was a tax collector. Sometimes he was dishonest and charged people more tax than he should have. He knew that this was not right. As a result, he did not have peace in his heart. He began to look for something better.

Zacchaeus heard about Jesus, but had not met him. One day as he sat at his desk, he heard that Jesus was coming to Jericho. The whole city was excited. The streets were crowded with people trying to catch a glimpse of Jesus.

Zacchaeus was so short that he could not see above the crowd. What should he do? He was determined to see Jesus. As he wondered, he saw the low branches of a tree nearby. Quickly he climbed up among the branches and waited. Soon he saw Jesus coming.

When Jesus came to the tree, Jesus stopped and looked up. Zacchaeus was looking for Jesus, and Jesus was looking for Zacchaeus! Jesus spoke. "Zacchaeus, come down immediately. I must stay at your house today."

The little man came down from the tree at once. He joyfully opened his home to Jesus. Jesus is always looking for needy sinners. When he calls, we must quickly answer, as did Zacchaeus. Receiving Jesus into his house was the first step. Receiving him into his heart would be the next.

We do not know how long Jesus stayed, nor do we know everything that was said. We can be sure that Jesus spoke kindly to him. He no doubt told him that God loves sinners; that his sins could be forgiven; and that he could be saved and have peace in his heart. Zacchaeus responded to Jesus' love and received him into his life.

Immediately Zacchaeus became a different person. The greedy and selfish heart became kind and compassionate. Instead of greedily wanting everything for himself, he now shared with the poor. He obeyed Jesus completely. He held nothing back. He even promised to repay those whom he had overcharged.

Jesus said, "Today salvation has come to this house." For the story in your Bible, see Luke 19:1-10.

Learning About Accepting Jesus
1. *How Do We Accept Jesus?*

A woman was asked if she knew how to be saved. "Oh, no," she answered, "only the educated can know how to be saved." This is not true. The steps to Jesus and salvation are simple to understand:

    a. Repent (turn from sin). Acts 2:37, 38.
    b. Believe (turn to Christ). Acts 16:31.
    c. Confess (tell others about faith in Christ). Romans 10:9.

Until the age of accountability a child is innocent. But even a child has a tendency toward sin. Thus at the age of accountability one needs to repent and turn from sin to the Savior. There are two roads which people travel. One road leads to hell, the other to heaven. These roads go in opposite directions. To be saved we must stop, turn around (repent), get on the right road, and follow Jesus.

Then there must be confession. If people do not believe in Jesus strongly enough to admit it with their lips, they do not *really* believe in him.

Read Revelation 3:20. Here it is clear that we receive Jesus as a person. It is possible to be baptized, to join a church, to agree with the rules of the church, to serve in the church, and still not be a Christian. If we have Christ in our lives, we are Christians; if we do not have him we are not Christians. Christianity is a relationship with a living person who knows, loves, strengthens, guides, and keeps. As soon as we sincerely invite Jesus into our lives he enters.

See Matthew 23:37 and John 5:40. Jesus can help only those who come to him for help. He can bless only those who receive him into their lives.

Dr. Walter L. Wilson tells of using John 3:16 to help a boy

receive Christ. He quoted the verse and stressed the word "gave." Showing the lad that Christ was God's gift, he asked, "Does the giving of a gift make it yours?"

The boy replied, "You must take it if it is to become yours."

"True," said the doctor, "and so Christ must be taken as God's gift, if he is to become yours. I am a doctor," he went on, "but I am not your doctor, am I?"

"No," said the lad.

"Why not?" asked the doctor.

"Because we never took you as our doctor," replied the boy.

"Very well, then, Jesus Christ is a Savior, but he is not your Savior unless you take him. Will you do so now?"

With bowed head, the boy told the Lord Jesus that he would take him as his Savior then and there.—*Sunday School Times.*

2. *We Accept Jesus as Savior.* Luke 23:39-43.

A preacher urged his hearers to accept Christ. He told them that to be saved they must accept him now. A man in the audience shouted, "What about the thief on the cross?" "Which one?" asked the preacher. The man who shouted felt that he could wait to receive Jesus until just before death. The story of the thieves who were crucified with Jesus shows that a man may be saved at the last minute. But it also shows that some people wait too long.

Every person who has not accepted Jesus as Savior is lost. We are saved only if by faith we invite him into our lives, and receive him as Savior.

3. *We Accept Jesus as Lord.* Matthew 16:24.

Some people want Jesus to save them, but they do not want him to lead them. They want to be their own "boss." A Christian receives Jesus as both Savior and Lord. Jesus will not be one without the other. He is either Lord of all or he is not Lord at all!

There is a throne in every heart. Before we become Christians we sit on that throne. When we accept Christ, we put him upon the throne and allow him to rule our lives. He then becomes

our Lord and Master. We do his will rather than our own. A. T. Pierson put it this way:

Look—Accept with the eyes.   *Hear*—Accept with the ears.
Come—Accept with the feet.   *Choose*—Accept with the will.
Take—Accept with the hands.   *Trust*—Accept with the heart.
Taste—Accept with the lips.   *Know*—Accept with the mind.

41

After Holman Hunt finished his great picture, *The Light of the World*, (see page 41), he asked a fellow artist to come and give his opinion on it.

After looking for some time, the artist exclaimed, "Why, Hunt, you have made a great mistake. There is no handle on the door. How can the Savior enter without a handle?"

"I have made no mistake," replied Hunt. "The handle is on the inside. The Savior cannot enter until the sinner himself opens his heart."

Questions About Accepting Jesus

1. What is the difference between believing with the mind and believing with the heart? James 2:19, 20.
2. Is repentance necessary for salvation? Luke 13:3.
3. Does God force anyone to become a Christian? Revelation 3:20.
4. How many ways are there to be saved? John 14:6.
5. What other words mean the same as faith?
6. How can we know we have real faith? Acts 19:18.
7. Can we love Jesus without obeying Him? John 14:15; 1 John 2:4.
8. Why is the gospel such good news? Luke 2:10, 11.

Reviewing the Lesson

Choosing the Best Advice

Henry asked his friends, "What must I do to be saved?" Here is the advice they gave him. It is not all good advice. Write the names of those giving the best advice.

_____   _____   _____

1. George said, "There are many ways to be saved. Choose the way you think best and stick to it."
2. Mary said, "It is not so important what you believe as long as you are sincere."
3. John said, "The only way to be saved is to turn from your sins and trust in Christ."

4. Bob said, "Only believe. How you live is not important."
5. Wilbur said, "Change your ways and go to church."
6. Sam said, "Why don't you wait until you are older?"
7. Jane said, "Believe on the Lord Jesus Christ and you will be saved."
8. Bill said, "To be baptized and keep the rules of the church is enough."
9. Carol said, "To be saved you must invite Jesus into your life."
10. Oren said, "Do the best you know and be kind to your neighbors."

Memory Verse

If you confess with your mouth, "Jesus is Lord," and believe in your heart that God raised him from the dead, you will be saved. For it is with your heart that you believe and are justified, and it is with your mouth that you confess and are saved. Romans 10:9, 10.

Day by Day with Jesus
First Day. I Am Sorry for My Sin.
Read Luke 22:54-62.
The Bible teaches two kinds of sorrow for sin. What are they? See 2 Corinthians 7:10.

1. _____ _____ brings repentance.

2. _____ _____ ____ _____ _____ brings death.

Judas and Peter are examples of these two kinds of sorrow or repentance. Judas was sorry and turned to suicide for relief. Peter was sorry and turned to God for forgiveness.

Repentance is not merely regretting something we have done. We may be sorry that we have been caught or that people have found out about our sin. This is not godly sorrow.

Johnny was arrested for breaking into a safe. The police discovered his fingerprints on the safe. In jail Johnny was asked if he were sorry for his sin. "I surely am," Johnny replied. "The next time I try a stunt like that, I'm going to wear gloves!" Johnny was not sorry he sinned against God, but that he was caught.

Second Day. I Confess My Sin.

Read Luke 18:13; 1 John 1:9.

Why must we confess sin? Because God wants us to realize that we are sinners. Until we do this, God cannot forgive us. Long ago a Christian named Augustine said, "The confession of evil works is the first beginning of good works." We must come right out and name our sins. It is not enough to pray, "O God, I am a sinner." We must get down on our knees and pray to God, "You know what a liar I have been and how I have been disobedient to my parents." In addition we must make things right with others. We should ask forgiveness of the person wronged. We should return the item stolen. This is called "restitution."

Take a sheet of paper. Make a list of your sins. Be willing to list them all; then confess them to God. Take the sheet of paper, burn it, tear it up, or throw it away. Remember, just as you destroyed the paper, so God has forgiven or taken away sins. God will remember them no more.

Third Day. I Repent of My Sin.

Read Luke 15:11-32.

The "prodigal son" knew he had done wrong. Was that repentance? At last he confessed his sin. But had he fully repented? Notice that he did not completely repent until "he got up and went to his father." He had to act. He had to turn his back on the old life and leave it.

Are you willing to forsake all the sins listed (on the sheet you destroyed) yesterday? If you are not willing, you have not truly repented on them. Ask God for a hatred for sin.

Fourth Day. I Look to the Savior in Faith.

Read Matthew 14:22-33.

Why did Peter sink? He was unable to walk on the water in

his own strength. Peter looked to Jesus when he began to sink. Peter did not call James or John or any of the other disciples in the boat to help. Only Jesus could help.

We must repent of our sins before we can be saved. But repentance does not save us. Jesus alone does that.

What does it mean to have faith in Jesus? It means to believe in him. But what does it mean to *believe?*

John G. Paton, a missionary in the New Hebrides, wanted to translate the Gospel of John into the language of the people. He found that there was no word in their language for *believe.* One day a native was sitting on a chair. His feet were on another chair. Dr. Paton heard him use one word which meant, "I am resting my whole weight on these two chairs." The word had been discovered! From then on he used that word for *believe.* So John 3:16 now read, "For God so loved the world that he gave his one and only son, that whosoever *resteth his whole weight upon him* shall not perish but have eternal life."

Try reading the following verses by using *rests his whole weight upon him* in place of believe: John 1:12; John 3:36; Romans 1:16.

Fifth Day, I Confess Him as My Savior.

Use your Bible to find who confessed Christ in each case. Fill in the blanks.

1. The Great Confession. Matthew 16:16 _____

2. Words of eternal life. John 6:68 _____

3. Spoken by a woman. John 11:27 _____

4. Spoken in a synagogue. Acts 9:20 _____

Sometimes people are received into the church without confessing Jesus with their lips. They stood in an evangelistic meeting, were instructed by the church, nodded their heads to the questions the minister asked at the baptism, but they never said with their lips—so that people could hear—"I believe that Jesus

Christ is the Son of God. I have taken him as my Savior." Every person should do this, not only once, but many times. Tell the next person you meet that you have received Jesus as your Savior.

Sixth Day. I Thank Him for Saving Me.
Read Luke 17:11-19.

Thank Jesus for saving you! How much do you appreciate salvation? Perhaps you have not given it as much thought as you should have. *Thanking* and *thinking* go together.

Ten lepers were healed by Jesus. Only one came back to thank him. Leprosy, in the time of Jesus, was a disease which could not be cured. Those who had it were not allowed to be with other people. They wore special clothes, lived in separate houses and could not enter inns, churches, mills, or bakeries. They were forbidden to touch healthy persons or eat with them. It was lepers like this that Jesus healed. They should have been thankful.

Sin is like leprosy. It, too, is a dreadful, incurable disease. Only Jesus can heal sin-sick people. He has healed you. Are you thankful? Have you ever told him so? Do it now!

Seventh Day. Salvation Is Free.
Read Ephesians 2:8, 9.

A young man came to a church meeting and earnestly asked, "What must I do to be saved?"

"You are too late," a worker said to the anxious young man.

"Don't say that. I want to be saved! I'd do anything or go anywhwere to get it."

"I cannot help it," replied the worker, "but you are too late. You see, your salvation was completed many hundred years ago by Jesus Christ. All you have to do is simply accept it. You have done nothing and can do nothing to earn it. Salvation is a free gift to all who repent and accept Jesus as Savior."

Working for Jesus
Be faithful in your projects. If you haven't already done so, begin item 15 on page 140.

The New Life

What Happened to Paul?

Paul was a different person. A few days earlier he had hated all Christians. "If I ever get hold of the Christians at Damascus, I'll put them in jail or I'll kill them," he likely muttered under his breath. "I'll get the necessary papers, make a trip to Damascus, and arrest them. Then I will bring them back to Jerusalem for punishment."

Paul, whose name was then Saul, had been busy in such work. He had arrested Christians, and tried to force them to give up their faith in Jesus. He said later, "I thought it was my duty to work against Jesus. I had many of his followers arrested in Jerusalem and put into prison. I went right into the synagogues and punished them. I tried to force them to say unkind, false things about Jesus. I was unreasonable about it. I acted like an insane person. When the Christians were put to death, I approved of it." Paul remembered the time Stephen was stoned. He had held the coats of those who threw stones. He had urged them on.

It is no wonder that Ananias was afraid when the Lord told him to visit Saul. "I have heard many things about this man," he said. "I have heard that he has done much evil to the saints at Jerusalem."

"Saul won't hurt you," the Lord told Ananias. "He is praying now."

When Ananias found Saul, at the house of Judas on Straight Street in Damascus, he found a changed Saul. Saul was converted. On his trip to Damascus he saw Jesus. The bright light from heaven made him blind. For three long days he refused to eat or drink. He was going through a struggle. Was he wrong after all? Should he turn from his old life and also become a follower of Jesus? At last the decision was made. When Ananias came, Saul gave his life to Jesus. He was able to see. He received the Holy Spirit and was baptized.

Now, instead of hating the Christians, Saul loved them. Instead of working against Jesus, he believed in him. Now he went to the synagogues to tell others about Jesus and to worship him. People could hardly believe their eyes. They said, "Isn't this the man who destroyed Christians in Jerusalem? "Isn't this the man who came to Damascus to arrest us?" It was Saul, but he was a changed man. He met Jesus, and Jesus made a new person of him. His heart was filled with love.

Learning About the New Life
1. *My Sins Are Gone!*

The Pilgrim's Progress is the story of a man who tried to rid himself of sin. For days he carried his sin like a heavy burden. At last he was told to go to the cross for help. This he did. As he stood before the cross in faith, the burden of sin fell from his back and rolled down the hill into a deep grave. It was never seen again.

Fill in the blanks to see what God does about our sin.

The blood of Jesus Christ _purifies_ us from all sin. _____1 John 1:7.

Jesus Christ _forgives_ our sins. Matthew 9:2.

Jesus Christ _takes away_ the sin of the world. John 1:29.

God said, "I will _remember_ their sins no more." Jeremiah 31:34.

When Jesus comes into a life, sin must go out. Jesus alone can take sins away. When he does, they are gone forever.

2. *I Receive a New Life.* John 3:3.

We need to be born again. The Bible tells us that we are dead in our sins. We need a new life. Salvation is the miracle of receiving new life. In the new life we love God. We love other people and are obedient to the teachings of the New Testament. The Bible calls this eternal life. It begins when we receive Christ.

"For if a man is in Christ he becomes a new person altogether—the past is finished and gone, everything has become fresh and new. All this is God's doing" (2 Corinthians 5:17, Phillips).

This is the result of the new birth. Thus the Christian life is not only a *new* life; it is also a *different* life; it is a *changed* life.

The New Testament is full of the stories of changed lives. Paul is only one example. Study the life of Peter to see the change in his life! But not all the conversion stories are found in the New Testament, for God changes lives today.

3. *I Am a Child of God.* John 1:12; 1 John 3:1-3.

The Bible calls followers of Jesus *children of God.* We are children of our earthly parents because we were born into their family. We are children of the heavenly Father because we were born into God's family.

The Bible tells us how we are related to God:

a. God is our Creator, we are God's creatures.

b. God is our King, we are God's subjects.

c. God is our Master, we are God's servants.

There is one more relationship that is the warmest and most beautiful of all:

d. God is our Parent, we are God's children.

Since we are all children of the same heavenly Father, we are therefore brothers and sisters. The book of 1 John tells us several times that we should love our brothers.

A reminder of the truth that we are all brothers and sisters in the church is *the holy kiss.* This ordinance is mentioned five times in the New Testament: Romans 16:16; 1 Corinthians 16:20; 2 Corinthians 13:12; 1 Thessalonians 5:26; 1 Peter 5:14. We are told to "greet one another with a holy kiss." You have no doubt seen persons in the church do this. It is often done with the foot washing ordinance—men with men, women with women. An ordinance, you remember, is an outward act which teaches an inner meaning.

The holy kiss teaches many things. It reminds us of the love in every Christian's heart for his brother, or sister in Christ. It also reminds us of the unity and fellowship that should be among believers as the family of God. The Bible says that the holy kiss should be observed by "all the brothers." We believe it is fitting that Christian women should greet Christian women, and Christian men should greet Christian men in this way.

4. *I Now Please God.* Romans 5:1; Romans 8:1.

These verses mean that when persons are in Christ Jesus we please God. Those who are not in Christ cannot please God. To be in Christ means to believe in him and receive him. Read John 3:36.

God destroyed the earth with a flood in the days of Noah. The only safe place, when the flood came, was the ark. It was God's method of saving the people. Noah and his family were saved because they believed God and, as a result, obeyed. They entered the ark; the rest of the people were lost. Noah pleased God, not because he lived a sinless life, but because he believed God and obeyed God.

In this connection read Acts 2:38. When a person receives Jesus, everything becomes new:

a. *One is born again*, one has a new life.

b. *One receives Jesus Christ*, one has a new person.

c. *One receives the Holy Spirit*, one has a new power.

Because we have a new life, Christians want to do the right.

Because we have a new person and power, Christians are able to do right, and thus able to live a life pleasing to God.

The Holy Spirit gives this power to Christians; he also *guides* (John 16:13), *counsels* (John 14:16-18), and *teaches* (John 14:26) every believer.

5. *The Love of God Is in My Heart.* 1 John 3:14, 15; 1 John 4:7, 8.

The one word which best describes the Christian life is *love*.

Christians love each other. In this connection we should study the ordinance of foot washing. Jesus gave Christians this ordinance to help them remember the importance of love, humility, and service. The story behind this ordinance is found in John 13.

In Bible times people wore sandals. After walking over the hot dusty paths, their feet became soiled. It was a kind and loving act to wash the feet of friends when they arrived at your house. Jesus taught, as he washed his disciples' feet, that all of us must engage in humble service. We must be loving and kind to our friends.

The night Jesus conducted the first communion service he also began the ordinance of foot washing. It's true that it was customary to wash the feet of guests when they arrived at a home. But this ordinance is not the continuation of an ancient act of courtesy. We must remember that in that last night, the disciples were arguing who would be the greatest among them.

Then Jesus, their Lord and master, took the place of a servant among them and washed their feet. He told them they should serve each other in the same way instead of striving for the highest places of honor. Jesus requested his followers to practice this simple service as a reminder of the importance of the love that leads to humility and service.

Christians even loves their *enemies*. Jesus also set the example in this. What did Jesus do when his enemies lied about him? made fun of him? beat him? spit upon him? and finally crucified him? See Luke 23:34. It is only when the love of God is in our hearts that we can love enemies.

Persons who are not Christians have a certain kind of love, but it is not Christian love. Their love is different from the love of God. People normally love only those who love them. God loves even those who do not love him. Our love is often for our own good. God's love is for the good of others.

The Mennonite Church believes in the way of love in all relationships. Jesus clearly taught that Christians must love enemies. Christians do not meet evil with evil but with good. They will not resist evil. They will not sue at law. They will always go the second mile in doing more than people ask of them.

Jesus taught Peter to lay his sword aside, because all who use the sword will perish with the sword. Furthermore, Jesus came to seek and to save people, not to destroy them; and his followers must do the same. Because his kingdom is not of this world, his followers will not engage in warfare.

We call this the way of *nonresistance*. When people mistreat us, we will love them, pray for them, and do good to them. We will not participate in the army or in warfare among nations. Christians love instead of hate, build instead of destroy, and turn from the guns and bombs of armies to the armor described in Ephesians 6:10-18.

Questions About the New Life
1. Can people convert themselves? Ephesians 2:4-9.
2. When does eternal life begin? John 3:36.
3. How do you explain Galatians 2:20? (You cannot live the Christian life; Christ lives it in you.)
4. How do Christians show others that they are disciples of Christ? John 13:35.
5. How does a person receive the Holy Spirit? Acts 2:38; Acts 5:32; Luke 11:13.
6. Does every Christian have the Holy Spirit? Romans 8:9.
7. What advice does Paul give? Ephesians 5:18.
8. Which of these sentences is correct? Romans 6:14.
   a. The Christian is not able to sin.
   b. The Christian is able not to sin.
9. How are young Christians like little children? 1 Peter 2:2.

Reviewing the Lesson
Check the things that belong to the new life.
   ✓ 1. I love everyone, even my enemies.
   ✓ 2. My sins are forgiven.
   ✓ 3. I am a changed person.
   __ 4. I am not interested in the needs of others.
   __ 5. I want to live like my ungodly neighbors.
   __ 6. I always want my own way.
   ✓ 7. The Holy Spirit lives in me.
   ✓ 8. I put Jesus first in my life.

52

___ 9. I am unkind to people who do not love Jesus.
✓ 10. I would rather suffer than do wrong.
✓ 11. God fills my heart with love.
✓ 12. I have peace in my heart.
✓ 13. I am not afraid to die.
___ 14. I enjoy looking at evil pictures.
___ 15. I have the cigarette habit.
✓ 16. I enjoy going to church.
✓ 17. I want to do the will of God.
___ 18. I am afraid of God.
___ 19. I worry myself sick.
✓ 20. I enjoy Bible reading and prayer.
___ 21. I swear when I become angry.
✓ 22. I gladly give my offerings.
✓ 23. I always tell the truth.
✓ 24. I love Jesus Christ.

Memory Verse
Therefore, if anyone is in Christ, he is a new creation; the old has gone, the new has come! 2 Corinthians 5:17.

Day by Day with Jesus
First Day. Some Big Words Explained.
Read Titus 3:5; Acts 15:3; Romans 4:25.

In these verses you will find some big words. We should understand the meaning of them. Look them up in the dictionary and write their meanings in the blanks. You may need to look under "convert" for converted, and "justify" for the meaning of justification.

1. Rebirth _____

2. Converted _____

3. Justification _____

These words all describe what happened to us when we received Jesus.

Second Day. Jesus Teaches the New Birth.

Read John 3:1-13.

How important is it to be born again? Read verses 5 and 7, and fill in the blanks.

1. Unless a man is born of water and the spirit, he cannot

_____ the kingdom of God.

2. You _____ be born again.

How can we be born again? You will notice as you read the Gospel of John that *believe* is the key word. The word is used dozens of times in one of its forms (believe, believes, believed, etc.). The way to be born again is to *believe*. Our part is to believe; God's part is to give new life. The new birth is God's miracle in our lives. Ask God to give you the new life. Believe that *God can do it*. Believe that *God will do it*. Then you can be sure that *God has done it.*

Third Day. Jesus Forgives Sin.

Read Luke 5:18-26.

The Pharisees asked, "Who can forgive sins but God alone?" They were right in raising the question. Only God *can* forgive sin. Because Jesus was God, he could do it.

A Christian doctor knew that some of his patients were too poor to pay. So he took red ink and wrote across their accounts, "Forgiven, unable to pay."

After his death, his widow found these unpaid accounts in the books. She said, "My husband has forgiven a lot of people. I could use that money now. I will try to collect it."

In the court the judge asked, "Is this your husband's handwriting?"

"Yes," answered the woman.

"Then," said the judge, "No court in the world can make these people pay."

In a similar way Jesus has forgiven the sins of those who come in repentance and faith. He *can* and he *has*. Thank him for forgivness.

Fourth Day. The Gift of the Holy Spirit.
Read Luke 11:9-13.
The Holy Spirit is a person. The Spirit should be spoken of as *he*, not *it*. The Bible speaks of being filled with the Spirit. Ephesians 5:18. Sometimes people have the mistaken idea that the Holy Spirit is like a substance which can be poured, like water. The Holy Spirit can think, feel, and desire.

1. Romans 8:27 speaks of his _____.

2. Romans 15:30 says the Spirit can _____.

3. Ephesians 4:30 tells us he can be _____.

Fifth Day. Signs of the Changed life.
Read John 15:1-8.
Only God can see what is on the inside of a person. We cannot see the inside, but we can see the outward acts. The outward acts tell us what is on the inside. A person with an evil heart will do evil deeds. The person who has been born again, and is changed on the inside, will do good deeds.

Jesus said that people are like trees. A bad tree bears bad fruit; a good tree bears good fruit. He said, "By their fruit you will recognize them." For the complete story, see Matthew 7:16-20.

In Galatians 5:22, 23 is a list of good fruit. These are signs of the changed life. Do you find them in your life? List them in the blanks:

The fruit of the Spirit is: _____, _____, _____,

_____, _____,

_____, _____,

_____, _____.

Sixth Day. Adopted into God's Family.
Read Romans 8:14-17. God is our parent.
1. We have been *born* into God's family.
2. We have been *adopted* into God's family.
What does Jesus say in John 15:16?

A little boy once came home from school crying because the other boys laughed at him. They said, "Your father is not your real father. You are only adopted."

When this boy's father heard about it, he said, "The next time the boys tease you, tell them that you are in our family because we chose you. Tell them that when they were born their parents had to take what they got."

God chose us not because we were better than other people, but because God loved us.

Seventh Day. Faith and Works.
Read Matthew 7:21-29:

Is it important to do the will of God? Are people saved by doing good works? Why should persons obey God? Christians obey God not to be saved, but because they are saved. They obey God because they love God.

Dr. Norman Harrison helped a nurse to understand that salvation is a gift. He said to her, "Suppose I tell you I will give you a gem worth ten thousand dollars. But you say, 'Excuse me, Dr. Harrison, I have only fifty dollars.' But you misunderstand. I am giving you the gem. It is yours for the taking. Now, if after receiving the ten thousand dollar gem I should ask you to take care of my child, would you do it?" Of course she would. This is where works comes in. They follow the gift of salvation.

Working for Jesus
Sometimes Christians are faithful for a while, but they soon become careless. The Lord wants Christians to continue to grow in the Christian life. Are you working with your projects? Are you faithful? Have you become tired of them? If you haven't started item 13 on page 140, you soon should.

Christian Assurance

Paul Knew He Was Saved

It is said that Paul was beheaded for his faith just outside the city of Rome. Paul knew he was to die, yet he was not afraid. Shortly before his death he wrote, "I am already being poured out like a drink offering, and the time has come for my departure I have fought the good fight, I have finished the race, I have kept the faith. Now there is in store for me the crown of righteousness, which the Lord, the righteous Judge, will award to me on that day—and not only to me, but also to all who have longed for his appearing." (2 Tim. 4:6-8).

Paul was not afraid to die. His sins were forgiven. All was well between him and God. He was sure of heaven. No wonder he was willing to suffer and die for his faith. 2 Corinthians 11 lists many things Paul suffered for Jesus' sake. Five times he was beaten with thirty-nine lashes. Three times he was beaten with rods; once he was stoned. Three times he was shipwrecked. Once he drifted at sea for a night and a day. Paul was often in danger. He knew what it was to be tired, cold, and hungry.

All these things he suffered because he lived for eternity instead of for time. He was willing to suffer on earth because he knew that the sufferings could not be compared with the glory he would experience in heaven with Christ. He trusted in Christ in life and in death. He trusted in Christ to take care of his body and his soul. He wrote, "But I am not ashamed, for I know in whom I have trusted, and I am confident that he is able to keep what I have entrusted to him until that day" (2 Timothy 1:12, Weymouth).

The secret of assurance is trust in God. If we trust in things of this world to save, we will learn to our sorrow that they will fail. If we look to people to save us, we will find that they also need a Savior. If we trust our own goodness to save us, we will someday learn that we are not "good enough" to please him. Only those who trust completely in God have salvation, peace, rest, and assurance.

Learning About Assurance

1. *Does God Want Me to Have Assurance?* 1 John 5:13.

Some people think it is wrong to say you know *now* that you are saved. They say that one cannot know until one dies, that the best one can do in this life is to hope. But the New Testament was written so that we might *know* that we have eternal life.

Bible saints knew that they were saved. David said, "The Lord is my shepherd." He did not say, "I *hope* the Lord is my shepherd, but I suppose I will have to wait until I die to find out for sure." He said, with confidence and assurance, that "the Lord *is* my shepherd" now.

Paul said, "For to me, to live is Christ and to die is gain." Death for Paul was not a "leap into the dark." Death for Paul meant personal fellowship with Christ. He did not *hope* and *guess* about his salvation. He was sure about it.

Church history tells of many Christians who were sure of their salvation. Thousands of them died rather than give up their faith. An example is John Ardly, whose enemies told him of the pain connected with burning at the stake. They wanted him to give up his Christian faith. But instead of recanting he replied, "If I had as many lives as I have hairs on my head, I would lose them all in the fire, before I would lose Christ."

2. *How Can I Be Sure?* 2 Timothy 1:12.

Paul was sure of his salvation. He said, "I know *whom* . . . he is able." Looking to ourselves for assurance is like casting an anchor into the bottom of a ship. If an anchor is to hold, it must be thrown outside the ship into the great ocean. It must go down into the water until it grips the rock itself. In the same way we must be anchored in Jesus if we are to be safe.

Paul was sure of his salvation because he gave his life to Christ. We may believe that the bank is a safe place to keep money. But until we are willing to deposit our money in the bank, we really do not believe it is safe. Paul handed his life over to Christ for safe keeping.

"But I don't feel saved," someone says. Salvation does not depend upon feeling. It depends upon faith in Christ. All those believing in Christ are safe. In the time of Noah all in the ark were saved. Those outside the ark were lost. The people inside the ark were not saved because they felt saved. Some of them may have trembled when the thunder crashed and the rain poured down. But they were saved because they obeyed and entered God's ark.

When we are saved, we can know it. We believe the promise of God. In addition there is the inner witness, the Holy Spirit, who tells our spirits that we are children of God. See Romans 8:16. But this witness is something different from feeling. It is true that when people are saved they often say, "I feel better." That is because the burden of sin has been taken away and they have a clear conscience. People who are truly saved have peace in their hearts.

3. *Am I Lost If I Sin?* 1 John 1:9; 2:1.

We are not lost because of specific sins, but because of our attitude toward sin. The Bible teaches that "no one who is born of God makes a practice of sinning" (1 John 3:9, Williams). When we as Christians sin, and are immediately sorry, we ask God for forgiveness. 1 John 1:9 promises us that God is faithful and just. God does two things for us: (1) God forgives and (2) God cleanses.

Christ loves us. He wants to see us live holy lives. We should remember that when we fall we are still in the family of God. A mother who is teaching her baby to walk does not throw the infant out the window when it falls. She helps the child up and starts it off again. God loves us more tenderly than any mother.

I am lost if I sin and refuse to repent. I am lost if I continue to live in sin and to practice it.

4. *Suppose I Can't Hold Out?* Jude 24.

We are as helpless to keep ourselves from sin as we are to save ourselves from sin. Only Jesus Christ saves us from sin and keeps us from it.

"Suppose, after the ark was completed God said to Noah, 'Now get eight great spikes of iron and drive them into the side of the ark.' And Noah got the spikes and did as he was told. Then the word came to him, 'Come, you and your whole family and hang on to these spikes.' And Noah and his wife, and the three sons and their wives, each grabbed hold of a spike. And the rains descended and the flood came, and as the ark floated on the waters their muscles were strained to the utmost as they clung to the spikes. Imagine God saying to them, 'If you hang on till the flood is over you will be saved!' Can you even think of such a thing as any one of them going safely through?"*

But how different the simple Bible story is! The Lord said unto Noah, "Go into the ark, you and your whole family." That is very different from holding on by their own effort alone. Inside the ark they were safe. Thus every believer who is in Christ loves him and as a result lives a life of obedient discipleship and is as safe as God can make him.

5. *Why Are Church Members Sometimes Not Sure?* Matthew 7:21-23.

These church members were lost because:

   a. They lived in sin.
      They did not do the will of the Father, v. 21.
      They were evildoers, v. 23.

   b. They put their confidence in something other
      than Jesus.
      They trusted in their confession, "Lord, Lord," v. 21.
      They trusted in their good works, v. 22.
      They did not know Jesus, v. 23.

Questions About Assurance
1. What is meant by assurance? See the dictionary.
2. How soon after conversion should I have assurance? Luke 19:9.

---

*H. A. Ironsides, *Full Assurance*, Moody Colportage Library, p. 101, adapted.

3. Must I know the date of my conversion in order to have assurance? 2 Timothy 3:14, 15.
4. Must I have assurance to be happy? Isaiah 57:20, 21.
5. Can I have assurance and later lose it? Matthew 14:29, 30.
6. How can I be sure that *all* of my sins are forgiven? 1 John 1:7, 9. Notice the word "all" in these verses.
7. Can I be good enough to get to heaven? Ephesians 2:8, 9.
8. What does the resurrection of Jesus have to do with my assurance? 1 Corinthians 15:17-20.

Reviewing the Lesson
True and False Statements
___ 1. God wants us to be sure of our salvation.
___ 2. I must wait until I die to find out whether I am really saved.
___ 3. After I am saved there is no danger that I will ever be lost again.
___ 4. It is possible to feel saved and still be lost.
___ 5. It is possible to get to heaven by being good and keeping the commandments.
___ 6. It is impossible to have assurance until at least five years after conversion.
___ 7. We are just as helpless to keep ourselves as we are to save ourselves.
___ 8. No one who is born of God makes a practice of sinning.
___ 9. We cannot depend on our *feelings* when it comes to our salvation.
___10. Paul was sure of his salvation because he had given his life to Christ.
___11. Jesus was never afraid because he trusted in God.

Memory Verse
I write these things to you who believe in the name of the Son of God so that you may know that you have eternal life. 1 John 5:13.

Day by Day with Jesus

First Day. Fear Is a Hindrance to Assurance.

Read Matthew 25:14-30.

Notice verse 25. The man said, "I was afraid." Fear prevented him from being his best.

Some years ago one of the world's longest bridges was completed at San Francisco. It cost seventy-seven million dollars. While building the first part of the bridge, no safety devices were used and twenty-three men fell to their deaths in the waters far below. In the construction of the second part it was decided to install the greatest safety net in the world, at a cost of one hundred thousand dollars. This net proved a great blessing. Now workmen could build without fear. Fewer men fell from the bridge (only ten; and they were saved by the net), and the work went from fifteen to twenty-five percent faster.

For God did not give us a spirit of timidity, a spirit of _____, of _____ and of _____. 2 Timothy 1:7

Think about Psalm 23. Ask the Lord to lead you by the hand and keep you.

Second Day. What If Doubts Come?

Read John 11:21-27.

A personal worker was leading a man to Christ. The worker said that the way to salvation is to accept Christ as Savior and to believe the promises of God. But the man kept replying, "I can't believe, I can't believe!"

"Who can't you believe?" asked the worker.

"Who can't I believe?" said the man.

"Yes, who can't you believe? Can't you believe God? He cannot lie."

"Why, yes," said the man. "I can believe God; but I had never thought of it in that way before."

Place these references in the right place: 2 Corinthians 1:20; 1 John 2:25; Titus 1:2.

1. God cannot lie. _____

The Golden Gate bridge at San Francisco

2. All the promises of God are yes._____

3. He has promised us eternal life._____
Ask the Lord for faith to trust in his promise.

Third Day. I Don't Feel Saved.

Read 1 Kings 19:1-8.

Elijah was discouraged. He was ready to give up. 1 Kings 18 tells of his great victory on Mt. Carmel. God had protected him from his enemies. Elijah's feelings ran high in chapter 18. When Elijah's feelings were low (1 Kings 19:1-8), he still had God very near. Elijah's feelings changed; God did not.

Martin Luther was once discouraged. His wife thought that she would try to help him. So one day when he came home, she

met him at the door dressed in a black dress—the kind that people wore when someone died.

"Who died?" Luther asked.

"God did," was the dreary reply.

"Kate, how can you say such a thing?"

"It must be true, my dear Martin, or you would not be so sad."

Martin learned the lesson. After this he trusted God and not his feelings.

Remember that every prayer should have in it thanksgiving.

Fact, Faith, and Feeling go walking on the fence. Faith keeps his eye on Fact and all goes well. Feeling follows. But when Faith takes his eye off Fact and turns around to see how Feeling is coming—both Faith and Feeling fall off the fence.

As long as a Christian (Faith) keeps one's eye on the promises of the Bible (Fact), all is well. Life is filled with peace and joy (Feeling). But as soon as a Christian takes one's eye away from the promise of God and God's Word and begins to examine one's feelings, a person will likely lose both faith and feeling.

When Christians look to Christ in faith, feelings will take care of themselves.

Fourth Day. Some Sure Promises
Read Hebrews 6:18, 19.
Professor Kellogg counted all the promises in the Bible. He found that there were 6,995. Promises from people to people, people to God, Satan to Jesus, and Father to Son numbered 4,186. There were 2,809 promises that God made to people. We can depend on every one of these 2,809 promises.
Here are a few. Match the reference with the promise.

___ 1. The promise of rest.   A. Romans 10:9
___ 2. The promise of peace   B. Acts 1:8
___ 3. The promise of salvation   C. John 14:27
___ 4. The promise of God's presence.   D. Matthew 11:28
___ 5. The promise of Holy Spirit power. E. Matthew 28:20
Read these promises. Make them yours.

Fifth Day. Take God at His Word.
Read Hebrews 11:1-6.
Satan wants people to question God's Word. Those with assurance today may have doubts tomorrow. How do you know you are saved; especially when doubts may arise? If we play with these doubts, we may fall into sin.
A Sunday-school teacher asked a little boy, "What is faith?"
He exclaimed, "Faith is believing God."
When Satan comes to tempt, stand on the promises of God! For example, read John 3:16. Who said it? Do you believe it? Then that should settle it. You have done your part. God will do his.
1. God said it.
2. I believe it.
3. That settles it.

Sixth Day. *Tests of Assurance.*

The letter of 1 John was written to help Christians *know* whether they have eternal life. Here are some tests which we can give ourselves. Draw a line to the correct sentence ending.

1. 1 John 2:3, "We know that we have come to know him
2. 1 John 3:9, "No one who is born of God
3. 1 John 3:14, "We have passed from death to life
4. 1 John 4:15, "If anyone acknowledges that Jesus is the Son of God,
5. 1 John 5:4, "Whatsoever is born of God

overcometh the world."
God lives in him and he in God."
because we love our brothers."
will continue to sin."
if we obey his commands."

Seventh Day. *Why Worry?*

Read Philippians 4:4-8.

Someone has said, "If you worry you don't trust; if you trust you don't worry." Should you worry about your salvation? Of course, if you are not right with God you should be worried, and should do something about it! But after you have given yourself to Jesus, you should believe that he will save and keep.

Surely, God is my _____; I will _____ and not be

_____. Isaiah 12:2.

One day a tourist lost his balance and fell into the Dead Sea. He could not swim and became very frightened. He struggled until exhausted. Then he noticed something strange. He did not sink, because the Dead Sea is so full of minerals that persons float on the surface of the water. In the same way, in our Christian life, the power of God is beneath us and around us to help us.

Working for Jesus

There is a great work for Christians to do in the world. Why did God save you? Perhaps he is calling you to serve as a missionary to speak to your neighbor about Christ.

J. W. Shank, a missionary to Argentina for many years, wrote this prayer: "I must understand, O God, why you saved me. I know you have a plan for me and I want to enter into your plan. I want to go where you say and I want to do what you ask of me. Amen." Do project 17 on page 140 this week.

Lesson 7

Church Membership

Christian at House Beautiful

John Bunyan wrote *The Pilgrim's Progress* more than 300 years ago. This is the story of a pilgrim who traveled from the City of Destruction (earth) to Mt. Zion (heaven). Each part of the story describes a phase of the Christian life. It tells how Christian (the pilgrim) was weighed down with a burden of sin, and how he lost his sins when he came to the cross. Most of the story tells of the joys and difficulties Christian experienced as he continued on his way to Mt. Zion.

Christian had a pleasant experience at House Beautiful. House Beautiful is an illustration of the church. Before Christian could enter, he had to prove to a girl called "Discretion" that he was a child of God by faith in Jesus Christ, and that he was a sincere Christian on his way to the heavenly city. Discretion was convinced of Christian's sincerity. She called to the door the rest of the family, who welcomed him into House Beautiful by saying, "Come in, blessed of the Lord; this house was built by the Lord of the hill, to entertain such pilgrims."

Once inside, Christian had joyous fellowship. Until supper was ready, they spent time sharing past experiences. Christian told his life story, how he journeyed to the cross and there lost his sins. He spoke of his temptations and how he had overcome them. One of the girls, Charity, asked him, "Have you a family?"

This made Christian sad, for he was reminded of his family, still in the City of Destruction, that would be lost if they did not come to Christ. Christian wept as he told of his wife and four children, unwilling to give up the pleasures of this world to come with him.

When supper was ready, the whole family sat down to a well-filled table. (This is an illustration of the communion service.) Now they no longer discussed the joys and sorrows of the way. All their talk at the table was about the Lord of the hill. They spoke lovingly of what Jesus had done and why he had done it. They sat at the table far into the night, speaking in detail of his love and his mercy.

Then they took Christian to his room. It was a large upper room with an east window. The name of the room was Peace. Here he slept till break of day. In the morning he was taken to the library where they were all encouraged as they read the stories of the faithful servants of bygone days. After a few days of this strengthening fellowship, Christian left House Beautiful and continued his journey.

What Is the Church?

The church is different from other organizations. Clubs or political groups are formed by people who have similar interests. The church is made up of people who have been "born" into it through accepting by faith Jesus Christ as Lord and Savior. The church is a spiritual fellowship; it is a divine society of persons "called out" to follow Jesus. The church does not belong to people. It belongs to Christ.

Learning About Joining the Church

The church began on the day of Pentecost. Acts 2 tells the story. On that day the Holy Spirit came and filled all the believers. Then Peter preached a powerful sermon. He told the large audience gathered in Jerusalem about Jesus' death on the cross. He told them that Jesus was no longer dead, but alive, and that God had made him both Lord and Christ.

1. *Read Peter's Sermon.* Acts 2.

Many listeners were unhappy because they realized they were sinners. Before people can be saved they must know they are lost. Jesus meant this when he said, "I have not come to call the righteous, but sinners to repentance (Luke 5:32)." Jesus is the Great Physician. Only those who realize that they are sick, sin-sick, feel the need of a physician.

The church is not a group of "good" people; it is a fellowship of "sinners" saved by grace.

2. What Did Peter Advise the People to Do? (Baptism)
Acts 2:38-41.

There must be an inner decision (repentance) and an outward expression (baptism) when joining the church. In Lesson 4 the necessary inner attitude in *Accepting the Savior* was studied. How well do you understand the meaning of baptism?

The Bible teaches many things about this ordinance. Look up the following references and fill in the blanks.

    a. Baptism is commanded.

    Matthew 28:19. Go and make disciples of all nations,

_____ _____ in the name of the _____,

and of the _____; and of the _____ _____.

    b. Repentance must come before baptism.

    Acts 2:38. Peter replied, _____ and be baptized....

    c. There are both water and Spirit baptism.

    Matthew 3:11. I baptize you with _____ for repentance:

but ... he [Christ] will baptize you with the _____

_____ and with _____.

    d. Baptism is a sign of entrance into the church.

    Acts 2:41. Those who accepted his message were

_____, and about _____

_____ were added to their number that day.

    e. Baptism stands for spiritual cleansing.

    Acts 22:16. Get up, be baptized and _____

_____ _____ _____, calling on his name.

Jesus gave us an example. Since he was baptized, his followers should also be baptized. Furthermore, he commanded his disciples to baptize all who believe in him.

Baptism stands for many spiritual truths. It speaks of the fact that believers are baptized by the Holy Spirit. It also means that the persons baptized publicly admit they have repented of and confessed their sins, have accepted Jesus as Savior, have had their sins washed away, and now have a clear conscience. 1 Peter 3:21.

In the past there has been much discussion about who should be baptized and about how baptizing should be done. Some churches baptize babies. However, we believe that only persons who have reached the age of accountability and who have accepted Jesus in repentance and faith should be baptized. An infant is innocent. A baby cannot repent, and cannot exercise faith.

Baptism also stands for entrance into the church of Jesus Christ. It is clear that infants cannot, assume the responsibilities of church membership. Thus they should not be baptized. Babies are in the love and care of Jesus until the age of accountability. Then they must choose to accept or reject him. Only those persons who have accepted him as Savior should be baptized.

As to how to be baptized, our church feels that pouring water on the head of the person to be baptized is an acceptable, Scriptural method.

3. *What Blessings Did the Early Church Provide for Her Members?* Acts 2:42.

Draw a line to the word which describes the phrase:

a. The apostles' teaching   Worship
b. Fellowship   Perhaps the communion service
c. Breaking of bread   Teaching and preaching
d. Prayer   Enjoying each other

Perhaps here we should note worship especially. There are two kinds of worship: private and public. We need both. There are times when we want to be alone with God. There are other times when we need to join with others in worship. Worship is one of the few things that we can do together. Public worship is more than a group of persons sitting together, each worshiping God separately. It is lifting our voices and hearts to God as one.

Worship is conversation between ourselves and God. God speaks through the Word, and by the Holy Spirit we answer in prayer. An important part of worship is reverence. This is a feeling of deep respect, love, and awe for God. To realize that God is present in every worship service will do much to enable one to behave properly.

4. *How Did Early Christians Treat Each Other?* Acts 2:44-46.

The first Christians lived like a big family. Christians have always needed and wanted the company of other Christians. In this they are like Jesus. He too wanted fellowship. He called twelve disciples to be with him. He often visited in the home of Mary, Martha, and Lazarus. Likely Jesus had this need for fellowship in mind when he planned the church.

An important word describes the way the early Christians functioned. This same word is used in Acts 1:14; 2:1; 2:46; 4:24; 5:12. Can you discover what it is?

When a person joins the church, he becomes part of the body of Christ. The members of the body love and protect each other. Whoever heard of one's own hand beating one's face? The hand protects the rest of the body. When the feet stumble and the body falls, the hands reach out to protect the body.

The early Christians were known for their love for each other. They enjoyed being together. They unselfishly shared their possessions.

In the early church, the members were well aware of the proper relationship among women, men, Christ, and God. The apostle Paul wrote about this in 1 Corinthians 11. He pointed out that God is head of all, then Christ, then man, then woman. Man is to show that he is taking his place in this order by worshiping with his head uncovered. In other words he would not take part in a Christian service with a hat or any other covering on his head. A woman reminds herself of her relation to man, to Christ, and to God by worshiping with her head covered. A covering or veil reminds us of this order. Paul also makes it clear that the covering of which he speaks is more than the woman's hair. In this connection, too, he speaks of a woman's hair as a glory to her. Paul taught that just as it was a shame for a woman to cut off her hair, so it was a dishonor to man, Christ, and God, for her to pray or prophesy with her head uncovered or unveiled.

5. *What Did the Unsaved Think About the Early Christians?*
Acts 2:47.

The early church was respected. Many people were attracted to this new way of life. People joined the church daily.

The new Christians not only lived a holy life before the people, but also they spoke about Jesus at every opportunity. They were concerned about the souls of others.

It is strange that the early church was respected and at the same time persecuted. But Jesus received the same treatment. Because the holy life of Christians makes unbelievers feel uncomfortable, they try to get rid of Christians. When evil persons have nothing more to say, they pick up stones. Acts 6, 7 tells the story of Stephen's murder. In Acts 6:10 we are told that his enemies "could not stand up against his wisdom or the Spirit by which he spoke." So they stoned him to death.

No doubt many of the people who watched Stephen die later

became Christians themselves. We know that one of them did. Who was he? See Acts 7:58.

Seven Questions to Answer

Here are some questions which are sometimes asked of persons as they are baptized and received into the church. Can you answer each one with a "yes"?

1. Do you believe in one true, eternal, and almighty God, who is the creator and preserver of all visible and invisible things?

2. Do you believe in Jesus Christ, as the only begotten son of God, that he is the only savior of mankind, that he died upon the cross, and gave himself a ransom for our sins that through him we might have eternal life?

3. Do you believe in the Holy spirit who proceeds from the Father and the Son; that he is an abiding comforter, sanctifies the hearts of believers, and guides them into all truth?

4. Are you truly sorry for your past sins, and are you willing to renounce Satan, the world, and all the works of darkness and your own sinful will and desires?

5. Do you promise by the grace of God, and the aid of his Holy Spirit, to submit yourself to Christ and his Word, and faithfully to abide in the same until death?

6. As you unite with the church, do you promise by the grace of God and the help of the Holy Spirit, to give and receive counsel from the members of this congregation and to live in loving fellowship with them? Will you support the congregation with your earnest prayers, regular attendance, loyal service, and faithful stewardship, as God gives you strength?

7. Since baptism is an act of identifying with Christ and his mission, do you now commit yourself to be his faithful witness and willing servant to needy and lost people everywhere?

Characteristics of the Church Member

Here are eight characteristics of the church member.* Can you explain the meaning of each one? Can you add to the list?

---

*Andrew R. Shelly, *Mennonite Weekly Review*, March 5, 1953.

1. *A Christian Member.* Acts 11:26; John 5:24; 1 Peter 2:24.
2. *A Growing Member.* 2 Peter 3:18; 2 Timothy 2:15.
3. *An Informed Member.* 2 Peter 1:5; 2 John 5:13.
4. *A Punctual Member.* 1 Corinthians 14:40.
5. *A Reverent, Worshiping Member.* Exodus 3:5; 12:27; 2 Kings 17:37, 38; Psalm 96:9; Matthew 2:2.
6. *A Tithing Member.* Malachi 3:8-10; Matthew 23:23; 2 Corinthians 8:9.
7. *A Separated Member.* Romans 12:1, 2.
8. *A Working Member.* Acts 1:8; 9:6; 1 Corinthians 12.

9. _____.

10. _____.
   A young man came to his pastor, asking to be received into the church. He said, "I want to be just a church member. I do not want to be a worker." The pastor replied, "The church has too many of that kind of members already."

Questions About Joining the Church
1. Who started the church? Matthew 16:18.
2. Which New Testament book tells the story of the first church?
3. What is the twofold task of the church? Matthew 28:19, 20.
4. How can the world recognize a true Christian? John 13:35.
5. What causes divisions in the church? James 4:1.
6. What is wrong with the Christian who substitutes radio or television for church attendance?
7. Can a person be a Christian without joining a church? Acts 2:46. See for an exception Luke 23:39-43.
8. Does water baptism save people? Acts 8:13, 22, 23.
9. Should babies be baptized? Acts 11:15-18; 10:47, 48.
10. Should everyone be baptized who asks for it? Acts 8:36-38.

Reviewing the Lesson
Fill in the blanks.

1. In *The Pilgrim's Progress* story, House Beautiful is an illustration of _____ _____.

2. Acts 2 tells the story of the beginning of _____ _____ on the Day of Pentecost.

3. _____ _____ founded or established the church.

4. Before people can be saved, they must realize that they are _____.

5. _____ and _____ are necessary before one is ready to be baptized.

6. According to Acts 2:42 the early church devoted themselves to _____ _____ _____, and _____, and _____ _____ _____ and _____.

7. The early disciples worked together and did everything with _____ and _____ hearts. Acts 2:46.

8. When we join the church we become part of the _____ _____ _____. 1 Corinthians 12:27.

9. When we join the church we promise to submit ourselves to _____ and his _____.

Memory Verse
"Those who accepted his message were baptized, and about three thousand were added to their number that day. They devoted themselves to the apostles' teaching and to the fellowship, to the breaking of bread and to prayer. Acts 2:41, 42.

Day by Day with Jesus

First Day. What Is the Church?
Read Matthew 16:16-19.

The church is made up of those who have made the same confession of faith in Jesus Christ as did Peter. The Bible gives many word pictures to help us understand what the church is. Some of these words are: house, body, and bride.

1. The church is a *house.* 1 Peter 2:5.

Jesus is both the builder and the foundation of the church. It is made up of living stones, Christians.

2. The church is a *body.* 1 Corinthians 12:27.

Christians are members of that body. Christ is the head. The hands, feet, etc., are members that take orders from the head as in a physical body.

3. The church is a *bride.* Ephesians 5:25-27.

The church is "engaged" to Jesus now. 2 Corinthians 11:2. Someday he will come to earth for his bride. The church will be "married" to him. Revelation 19:7. We *love* Jesus and he *loves* us.

Thank God for the living church of which we are a part.

Pray for the projects you are working on each week.

Second Day. Fellowship in the Church.
Read Acts 2:41-47.

Jesus taught his followers to observe several practices which would always remind them of the blessing of church fellowship. We have studied these ordinances before. Here is a good review:

1. Fellowship in the *Lord's Supper.* 1 Corinthians 10:17.

"We, who are many, are one body, . . . one loaf." Just as the many grains of wheat are crushed and made into one flour and finally into one loaf of bread, so we being many members are one fellowship in Christ. We are reminded of this great truth when we eat the bread in the Lord's Supper or communion service.

2. Fellowship in *Foot Washing.* John 13:14.

Jesus said, "You also should wash one another's feet." As Christians, we are all on the same level. We are to think of ourselves as servants of each other. This should be true not only when we wash feet, but in our everyday living. Foot washing is a reminder of this duty.

3. Fellowship in the *Holy Kiss.*

Five times in the New Testament we are commanded to greet each other with a holy kiss. Romans 16:16; 1 Corinthians 16:20; 2 Corinthians 13:12; 1 Thessalonians 5:26; and 1 Peter 5:14.

The holy kiss may be observed with foot washing and at other times when we wish to remind ourselves that we are all brothers and sisters in the family of God.

Thank the Lord for Christian fellowship. Pray for love to all the believers.

Third Day. Worship in the Church.

Read 1 Corinthians 11:1-16.

As you worship today ask these two questions:

1. What did God say to me?
2. What did I answer back?

Ask the same questions as you worship at church next Sunday. The Valiente Indians, in their Bible, describe the heart which worships as "cutting itself down before God." Like a tree in the forest falls under the woodman's ax, so the worshiper falls low before God.

Read this chapter carefully and be ready to discuss with your pastor how it is interpreted in your congregation.

Fourth Day. Caring for Each Other in the Church.

Read Romans 12:9-21.

The church is bound together like a family. A good family is a unit. If Willie comes down with appendicitis, his parents don't get out the family account book and figure out how much Willie has been worth to the family, in dollars and cents, in his eight years of life.

Suppose they figure that his services, such as they were—wiping dishes, sweeping sidewalks, taking out the garbage, or what not—had been worth about $62.75 since the last time he was sick. They wouldn't send Willie to the hospital with a note to the doctor: "Please give our Willie $62.75 worth of operation. That's all he has put into the family budget and that's all we're going to let him take out!"

Not by any means. Willie is taken to the hospital and whatever operation he needs, that is what his parents want him to have, even if it costs 20 times what Willie has been worth in cash. The family gives Willie what he needs, and they expect him to help out in all the ways he can.

Ask the Lord to help you to be a real brother or sister in the church. Go and visit one of the church members who is old or sick.

Fifth Day. I Need the Church.
Read 1 Corinthians 12:12-26.

God made people so that they need each other. God said, "It is not good for the man to be alone." Sometimes people say they can be Christians alone, and that they do not need the church. So they stay at home on Sunday morning and watch a television preacher instead of going to church. But the Bible says Christians should "not neglect meeting together as some do, but let us encourage one another" (Hebrews 10:25, Goodspeed).

People who refuse to join the church and attend its services, generally lose out in the Christian life.

Have you ever built a fire in the woods? It is difficult to get one stick to burn alone. But if kindling is placed under a whole pile of sticks they warm each other and burn more brightly.

I need the church to encourage me, to teach me, and to give me opportunities for service.

Give thanks for God's wisdom in planning the church.

Sixth Day. The Church Needs Me.
Read Romans 12:3-8.

It is true that God can get along without us. But it is also true that when we do not help God, God's work suffers. God works through us.

A field left to itself will grow up in weeds and briars. But when people cooperate with God, when they plow, plant, and cultivate, wonderful crops can be grown. God likewise needs people to work in the church. God needs teachers, leaders, and workers of all kinds. The same Jesus who called the Twelve is calling us today. Jesus wants more to answer his call. He said, "The harvest is plentiful but the workers are few" (Matthew 9:37).

Will you answer His call to work in the church?

Seventh Day. The Church Is a Lighthouse.
Read Matthew 5:14-16.

For hundreds of years, storm-driven sailors have looked for lights to warn them that land or dangerous rocks were near. Early peoples along the southern Mediterranean built towers from which they hung metal baskets with burning coal or wood. Modern lighthouses have large lights which can be seen twenty miles away.

The church is like a lighthouse. It warns the people of spiritual danger and shows them which way to go. Christians should be concerned about the welfare of others. The church is in the world for a reason. God wants to see the unsaved come to Jesus, the *light of the world*. We who are Christians are also lights. People watch us and follow us.

Be careful to lead them in the right direction.

Working for Jesus

A study of Acts shows that the early Christians were workers in the church. They not only enjoyed the blessings of God themselves, but they wanted to share their newfound joy with others. This week carry out project 2 on page 140.

How to Grow
in the Christian Life

How George Müller Grew Strong

George Müller was a man of God. He became known as one of the greatest people of prayer in history. Without asking anyone but God for money, he raised $7,000,000 in his lifetime to build and run a large home for orphans at Bristol, England. At the age of seventy, Mr. Müller began to make great preaching tours. Three times he traveled through the United States in his missionary work. He died in 1898 at the age of ninety-four.

But George Müller was not always a saint. As a youth he lived a wicked life. The night his mother lay dying (when George was fourteen), he played cards until two in the morning. The next day, a Sunday, he went to a tavern with some of his friends and got drunk. He said, I became worse and worse." He was guilty of lying, stealing, gambling, and almost every kind of sin.

How then was it possible for George Müller to ever become a strong Christian?

It did not happen all at once.

He first of all felt a need. He was unhappy in his sin. He said, "I had no enjoyment in it, and I could see that I would someday come to a miserable end."

Then one evening George went to a prayer meeting. Of this meeting he wrote, "The Lord began a work of grace in me." His life was changed. He wanted to do the right, but he was still weak. He said, "My wicked companions were given up; the going to taverns was discontinued; I no longer made it a habit to tell lies, but still told some untruths. I now no longer lived habitually in sin, though *I was still often overcome* and sometimes even by open sins."

Here are several reasons George grew in his Christian life:

1. *He allowed God to work.* He said, "I read the Scriptures, prayed often, loved the believers, went to church from right mo-

tives, and stood on the side of Christ, though laughed at by my fellow students."

2. *He made wise decisions.* After his conversion George fell in love with a non-Christian girl. She took the place of Christ in his heart. When he realized what was happening, he gave up the girl. "It was at this time," he says, "that I began to enjoy the peace of God, which passes all understanding."

3. *He gave himself fully to God.* This happened when George was twenty-four years old and after a severe illness (1829). In a letter near the close of his life he wrote, "I became a believer in the Lord Jesus in the beginning of November, 1825, sixty-nine years ago. For the first four years I lived a very weak Christian life. But in July, 1829, now sixty-six years ago . . . I gave myself fully to the Lord. Honors, pleasure, money, my physical powers, my mental powers, were all laid down at the feet of Jesus, and I became a great lover of the Word of God. I found my all in God."

4. *He worked for God.* When George first asked God for money, it was as hard for him to trust in God for a quarter as it was afterwards to trust him for a thousand dollars. The more he exercised his faith, the stronger it became.

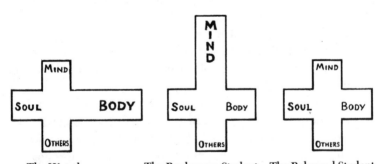

The Wrestler   The Bookworm Student   The Balanced Student

Learning About Growing Strong

1. *How Should We Grow?*

   a. *We should grow in a balanced way.* Luke 2:52. To be the kind of person that pleases God we must grow physically, mentally, socially, and spiritually. If we are interested only in building strong bodies to the neglect of Bible-reading and worship, we become unbalanced. If we are interested only in books and study—never giving our bodies the needed exercise for health, or never mixing with people—we are again unbalanced.

How does 2 Peter 3:18 tell us to grow?

b. *We should grow through fellowship.* Colossians 3:12-16. Fellowship is a sharing of life. It is both giving and taking. It is more than several persons simply meeting at a certain place. Fellowship with Christian friends brings the best out of us. Robert Louis Stevenson said, "When I met him I was looking down; and when I left him, I was looking up." A Christian friend will do that for us.

Fellow believers encourage, comfort, and strengthen us. As Christian teachers teach us the Bible, we are built up. The good example of a fellow Christian makes us want to do better.

George Müller gave himself to the Lord when he saw a young missionary give up all the luxuries of a beautiful home for Christ. This revealed to Müller his own selfishness.

c. *We should grow through Bible reading.* Acts 17:10, 11; 2 Timothy 3:16, 17. Were the Bereans satisfied to get the Bible secondhand through Paul and Silas?

How often did they read the Bible?

Read 2 Timothy 3:16, 17. List four things the Bible is good for:

_____, _____, _____, _____.

Bible study makes the Christian complete. It gives us strength for service.

The words of God are food for the soul. As we read the Bible and thinks about it, it becomes part of us—just as food becomes part of the body. This is a wonderful thing. We cannot understand it. Scientists still do not understand how the food we eat it turned into bones, eyes, lungs, and skin. But we do not wait to eat bread and meat until we understand how God makes it a part of our bodies. Neither do we wait to read the Bible until we understand how God uses it to change our lives.

d. *We should grow through prayer.* Luke 11:1-13. Prayer is exercise. Prayer is work. It is often an inward struggle, a wrestling with our sins and selfishness. Prayer does not come easily. It takes effort. It means listening as well as speaking.

David Brainerd was a missionary to the American Indians over 200 years ago. He spent several hours a day in prayer to God. At times he prayed so earnestly that he was wet with sweat. God worked through David Brainerd. Many Indians were saved.

Prayer is looking at Jesus. When we look at Jesus, He changes our lives. The change is gradual. The more we look at him, the more we become like him. 2 Corinthians 3:18. Have you ever read the story, "The Great Stone Face," by Hawthorne? It is the story of a boy who spent hours looking at the likeness of a man's face, made by the rocks up in the mountains. According to the story, when the boy grew to manhood he himself looked like the man in the mountains. He had looked at the face so long that he became like it.

e. *We should grow through giving.* 2 Corinthians 8:1-9. The Macedonians were very poor. Yet when Paul told them of the need in the Jerusalem church they wanted to help. Paul told them not to feel pressured, but to give as much as they wished. The Macedonians gave more than was expected and were blessed. Paul encouraged the Corinthian church to grow in giving as they had in the other graces, such as faith, knowledge, and love.

We cannot give too much. The Bible says that poor planting means a poor harvest, and generous planting means a generous harvest. 2 Corinthians 9:6.

Elijah once asked a poor widow to share her last handful of flour and her last bit of oil. This she did. The result was that she had more than before. God multiplied her flour and oil. God blesses people who give liberally.

A certain farmer who was known to be a generous giver was told by his neighbors, "We cannot understand you; you give more than any of the rest of us, and yet always seem to have more to give."

"That's easy to explain," replied the farmer. "I keep shoveling into God's bin, and God keeps shoveling more and more back into mine; and God has the bigger shovel."

The greatest blessings received are spiritual. Giving brings joy and increased interest in the work of the church. When we give we lay up treasure in heaven; we think more about heaven.
f. *We should grow through service.* 1 John 3:16-18. For growth there must be activity and exercise. The muscles of the arm are strengthened by swimming, weight-lifting, tennis, or any work in which the arms are used. The muscles of the leg improve from bicycling, running, jumping, or walking. Everyone needs some physical exercise to be healthy and strong.

When certain parts of the body are not used, they become weak. A Hindu, Faquir Agastiya, of Bengal, India, held his arm up for ten years (1902-1912) until a little bird built its nest on the palm of his hand. He did it because of his religious belief. The first three months he suffered terrible pain. After that the arm became stiff and useless and finally so fixed that it was impossible for the man to lower it.

Jesus once told the story of a man who wrapped his money in a napkin, and hid it in the earth, instead of using it for God. The result was that the man's money did not increase and, in the end, it was taken away from him because he did not use it.

In the Christian life we grow by doing. Our love grows when we love. We become better teachers as we teach. We become stronger personal workers as we witness.

2. *What Can We Do to Help Our Growth?* 1 Peter 2:2.

We cannot make ourselves grow, but we can furnish and supply those things necessary for growth.

A healthy, growing body needs the right kind of food. One needs proteins, minerals, and vitamins as well as sugars, fats, and starches. One also needs plenty of exercise, fresh air, and rest.

What do we need for spiritual growth?
a. *We need to read the Bible.* The Bible is food to the soul.
b. *We need to pray.* Prayer has been called the vital breath of the Christian.

c. *We need to work for Jesus.* Service is soul exercise.

d. *We need the fellowship of other Christians.* Christians strengthen one another. When we help others, we help ourselves.

A man was lost in a snowstorm. He was exhausted and ready to give up, when he stumbled upon another man in the snow. What should he do? He was too tired and cold to help the man, and yet he could not leave him there to die. He decided to carry the unconscious man as far as he could on his back. As he walked along the added effort warmed him. The warmth of his body revived the man on his back. Soon he became conscious and could walk. Together they battled the storm, helping each other to a place of shelter.

e. *We need to keep ourselves from evil.* Christians, with God's help, must separate themselves from all the things of this life that are evil. Earlier we studied about Satan and his kingdom. The Bible helps us to identify the evil works of Satan, such as unbelief, disobedience, pride, lying, swearing and evil speech, dishonesty and stealing, murder, immodest clothing, jewelry, sinful amusements, immorality, and covetousness.

Followers of Jesus have nothing to do with these evil practices, for to love these things is to be an enemy of God. It is impossible to serve two masters. The Christian is to live as Jesus lived and to obey his teachings. The work of the church fills a central place in life. Fellowship with other Christians is a joy.

Christians must always keep close to Christ. They must guard against joining organizations in business, politics, or school that would lead to pride or otherwise harm spiritual growth. They must guard against temptations to follow the patterns of non-Christians in immodest dress, wearing of jewelry, and fashionable hair styles. They must guard against the improper use of leisure time that allows one to become absorbed in the commercial amusements of the day.

The fact is, we become different from the world only as we allow the Holy Spirit to make us more like Jesus.

f. *We need to keep ready for the Lord's return.* The Bible teaches that Jesus will return again. Acts 1:11. No one knows the time of His return. Matthew 24:36. Because of this it is important that Christians be ready for His return at all times. Matthew 24:44. Perhaps you have read the old motto: "Do nothing you would not like to be doing when Jesus comes; say nothing you would not like to be saying when Jesus comes; go nowhere you would not like to be when Jesus comes."

The coming of Jesus for Christians will be joyous. We will meet old friends. Together we will become like him. 1 John 3:1. John wrote, "Everyone who has this hope purifies himself, just as he [Christ] is pure" (1 John 3:3). For non-Christians the coming of Jesus will be a fearful time of judgment. 2 Thessalonians 1:7, 8.

In connection with the coming of Jesus there will be other great events. When they will occur and in exactly what order is not clear. But we are sure that Jesus will come again. We are sure that the bodies of both good and evil people will be raised from the dead. John 5:28, 29. There will also be judgment. People from all nations will appear before God. Matthew 25:31, 32. Paul wrote, "We must all appear before the judgment seat of Christ, that each one may receive what is due him for the things done while in the body, whether good or bad" (2 Corinthians 5:10). The true followers of Jesus will not be condemned, but those who do not serve God will be punished. Revelation 20:15.

Therefore, we must live so that we are always ready either to meet him in his second coming, or to meet him in death should we die before he comes.

Questions About Growing Strong
1. Is it possible to grow in love? Philippians 1:9.
2. Can one grow in faith? 2 Thessalonians 1:3.
3. Does the Lord expect us to be fruit-bearing Christians? John 15:8.
4. What kind of fruit does the growing Christian bear? Galatians 5:22, 23.
5. What is necessary if we would be growing, fruit-bearing Christians? John 15:4, 5.
6. Did Paul think that he had finished growing as a Christian?

Philippians 3:12. (Phillips translates it, "I do not consider myself to have 'arrived,' spiritually, nor do I consider myself already perfect. But I keep going on.")

7. Does the kind of books and magazines we read have anything to do with our growth? Philippians 4:8; Proverbs 23:7.
8. To whom do we look as our ideal and goal? Ephesians 4:13.
9. How can we measure our spiritual growth?
10. How may persecution or sickness cause Christian growth?

Reviewing the Lesson

How to Grow Strong in Christ
(Check the correct ways)

__ 1. Receive new life from Christ by being born again.
__ 2. Remove hate, jealously, and all other hindrances to growth.
__ 3. Have nothing to do with other Christians.
__ 4. Decide to take yourself in hand and to grow.
__5. Read the Bible every day.
__ 6. Pray for yourself and others.
__ 7. Be loving and helpful to others.
__ 8. Be active in the work of the church.
__ 9. Share your Christian experience with others.
__10. Allow the Holy Spirit to work in your life.
__11. Look to Jesus as your example and ideal.
__12. Spend some time each day watching soap operas.

Memory Verse

But grow in the grace and knowledge of our Lord and Savior Jesus Christ. To him be glory both now and forever! Amen. 2 Peter 3:18.

A PRAYER FOR GROWTH

More holiness give me, more strivings within;
More patience in suffering, more sorrow for sin;
More faith in my Savior, more sense of his care;
More joy in his service, more purpose in prayer.

More gratitude give me, more trust in the Lord;
More pride in his glory, more hope in his Word;
More tears for his sorrows, more pain at his grief;
More meekness in trial, more praise for relief.

More purity give me, more strength to o'ercome;
More freedom from earth-stains, more longings for home;
More fit for the kingdom, more used would I be;
More blessed and holy, more, Savior, like thee.

—P. P. Bliss

Day by Day with Jesus
First Day. Why Should We Grow?
Read Luke 2:52; 2 Peter 3:18.
1. Because *Jesus grew.* Luke 2:52.
2. Because *God wants us to grow.* 2 Peter 3:18.

All living things grow. A person cannot grow spiritually unless one is alive. Before one can grow spiritually one must be *born again.* This is the starting point. New Christians are called "babes" in the Bible.

The Lord expects young Christians to grow spiritually just as all parents expect their babies to grow physically and mentally. Have you ever seen a baby that does not grow? Sometimes Christians do not grow. They are "babes in Christ" after being in the church many years. God needs strong Christians to work for him and to help others. Babies cannot help others; in fact, they can't help themselves.

Second Day. How Jesus Grew.
Read Luke 2:52 again and Ephesians 4:14-16.
Fill in the words that tell how Jesus grew:

1. Mentally _____

2. Physically _____

3. Spiritually _____

4. Socially _____

Jesus was a balanced person. He studied and learned. He took care of his body. He spent much time in prayer. He loved people and liked to be with them.

Third Day. Joined to Jesus.
Read John 15:4-8.

There can be no growth without remaining in Jesus. How often is the word "remain" used in these verses? To "remain" means to "stay." Christians cannot grow and bear fruit unless they remain or stay in Jesus and receive strength from him. How much does Jesus say we can do without him? How long would a branch grow if it were cut from the vine? How much fruit would it bear?

An electric motor is useless unless it is plugged in. It can do no work and has no strength alone. Sometimes Christians try to run on their own power. But they always fail. They must live close to Jesus to be strong and grow. People are joined to Jesus when they say "yes" to him and invite him into their lives. Christians must stay joined to him if they are to grow.

Fourth Day. Babies Should Grow.
Read Hebrews 5:12-14.

Babies cannot eat heavy foods. They must drink milk. Small babies cannot feed themselves nor others.

New Christians are much like babies. At first they can understand only the simple Bible teachings (milk). As they study and grow spiritually they are able to understand the deeper Bible truths (meat). At first they need to be taught. As they grow stronger they are able to teach.

Sometimes people still need to be milk-fed when they should be meat-eaters.

Fifth Day. Who Makes Us Grow?
Read Matthew 6:27; 1 Corinthians 3:7.

1. We cannot make ourselves grow. Matthew 6:27.
2. Only God can bring about growth. 1 Corinthians 3:7.

Growth is a mystery. We can watch things grow, but we cannot make them grow. We can sow an apple seed but we cannot make the seed sprout. We cannot make the little apple tree grow leaves, become a big tree, blossom, and produce apples. Only God can cause the growth of the tree. The same thing is true of our souls. God alone can make us grow spiritually.

Sixth Day. *What Keeps Us from Growing?* 1 Peter 2:1-9.

When a farmer gets a field ready for planting, he takes out the thorns, weeds, and stones. He tests the soil to see if it has too much acid or too much alkali. After the plants come up, he watches them to see that no disease or pests damage them.

There are also certain things which keep people from growing spiritually. These things need to be removed from one's life. See 1 Peter 2:1, for the words defined here, and write them in.

1. Desire to harm others _____

2. Crafty, tricky _____

3. To pretend to be what one is not _____

4. To be jealous or resentful _____

5. Speaking to do harm _____

Seventh Day. *Growth in Love.*

Read 1 Corinthians 13.

Jesus said, "All men will know that you are my disciples if you love one another" (John 13:35). One of the greatest evidences of Christian growth is a loving spirit. There is no substitute for love. 1 Corinthians 13:1-3. Love expresses itself in many ways. 1 Corinthians 13:4-7. Love never fails and will continue throughout eternity. 1 Corinthians 13:8-13. Check your life by this chapter.

Working for Jesus

Growth expresses itself in loving behavior at home. Carry out project 4 on page 140 not only this week, but also in all the weeks to come. Project 15 should be well developed by now.

Lesson 9

How to Overcome Temptation

How Jesus Overcame Temptation

In 1927 Charles A. Lindbergh made the first solo flight across the Atlantic Ocean. Immediately he became a great hero. Everyone wanted to see him. More than 100,000 people gathered at the airfield in Paris to greet him. The *New York Times* newspaper ran a fifteen-page story of the event. Everyone wanted to read about him, about his dangerous flight through fog, sleet, and rain. Everyone admired the courage of the young 25-year-old pilot who made the 3600-mile flight successfully.

But the greatest man of all time is Jesus. He was the first to win a complete victory over Satan. Jesus did not sin. He did not yield to temptation. He won every battle with Satan. How did he do it? There are three secrets of Jesus' spiritual success.

1. *Jesus Believed in God.* He believed that God loved him. He believed that God's way was the best way. When Satan suggested a way different from God's, Jesus refused to listen. Jesus did not doubt or wonder what he should do, because he loved God and was fully devoted to God. "This is the victory that has overcome the world, even our faith" (1 John 5:4). Jesus had perfect faith in God.

2. *Jesus Was a Person of Prayer.* Jesus often went into the mountains to pray. He prayed early in the morning (Mark 1:35); he prayed all night (Luke 6:12); he prayed when tempted (John 6:15); and he prayed before he went to the cross (Matthew 26:36). The cross (trial and death of Jesus) was his greatest temptation. But Jesus won the victory because he lived close to God.

3. *Jesus Used the Word of God.* Turn to Matthew 4:1-11. How many times was Jesus tempted? How many times did he reply to Satan with quotations from the Old Testament? ("It is written.") It is surprising that Jesus, the Son of God, repeated

verses from the Old Testament. He could have spoken directly to Satan in his own words. Perhaps he wanted to be an example to us today.

Learning About Overcoming Temptation
1. *How Does the Devil Tempt Us?* Genesis 3:1-5.
The devil makes suggestions. He suggests that his way is the best way to live. He urges us to disobey God and God's Word. He tempts through eyes, ears, nose, feelings, and even minds. He calls attention to things God does not want us to have or to do. The devil is a liar, and the good which he promises never comes. Those who do as he says are always unhappy.

When we become Christians, we choose to obey Jesus as our Master. Suppose your job is to carry bags of groceries to customers' cars. One day, while walking down the street with a bag of groceries, the hardware merchant calls out his front door, "Come in and work for me. To begin, I want you to sweep my floor." Immediately you reply, "I'm sorry, but I'm working for someone else. I can't stop now." Jesus is our Master. We take orders from him only.

2. *Dare We Blame All Temptation on the Devil?* James 1:14.
It is natural to blame others for our mistakes and sins. Whom did Adam blame for his sin? Whom did Eve blame? Some people even blame God when they are tempted. God tests people; the devil tempts them. God wants to see us stand; the devil wants to see us fall. God says, "Here are two ways. Choose the high way." The devil says, "Here are two ways. Choose the low way."

Not all temptation comes from without. Some of it comes from within. Our inner desires pull us away from God. James calls it "desire."

We dare not blame the devil for all our mistakes. Sometimes we must blame ourselves. Adam blamed Eve, and Eve blamed the serpent. But God held them both responsible and punished them both.

After Jesus saves us, we have a new self. The old self is still there, but we must not listen because the old self draws us away from God. We must act as though the old self were dead. Paul says we should be dead to self and sin but alive to Christ and his will for our lives.

3. *Can Evil Companions Lead Us into Sin?* Proverbs 1:10; 16:29.
William E. Gladstone, at one time the Prime Minister of Great Britain, said to a group of young men who asked him for suggestions on how to make a success of life: "Choose wisely your companions, for a young man's companions, more than his food or clothes, his home or his parents, make him what he is."

The story of many prisoners is that they got into wrong company. Evil companions took them first to wrong places and then into sinful practices.

When John Wesley was a student at Christ Church, Oxford, he decided to choose only those friends who would help him on the road to heaven. Remember, we can't always choose our surroundings, but we *can* choose our friends! Christians must be kind and friendly to wicked people, but cannot join them in doing evil.

4. *Must a Christian Sin When Tempted?* 1 Corinthians 10:13.
This verse tells us several things about temptation.
a. There is nothing unusual about temptations.
b. In temptation we can depend on God to help.
c. God allows us to be tempted.
d. God limits temptation to what we can stand.
e. God always makes a way out for us.
The Christian can never say, "The temptation was so great, I had to yield."

5. *What Spiritual Weapons Has God Furnished?*
Ephesians 6:10-18.
We cannot win the battle in our own strength. We must use the spiritual equipment which God has given us. Fill in the missing words.

The Armor of God

The belt of _____

The breastplate of _____

The shoes of _____

The shield of _____

The helmet of _____

The sword of _____

The "secret" weapon (v. 18) _____

It is impossible for us to have spiritual victory without Bible reading and prayer. Martin Luther said, "If I fail to spend two hours in prayer each morning, the devil gets the victory through the day. I have so much business I cannot get on without spending three hours daily in prayer."

6. *Who Gives Us Victory?* 1 Corinthians 15:57.

We have victory through Jesus Christ. He is the only one who is able to overcome Satan. We are too weak. No one else is able, because all have sinned. Only when Jesus lives in us we can win the victory over temptation. A little girl once said, "When Satan knocks at the door of my heart, I send Jesus to the door."

When Jesus comes in, sin goes out. A college boy had several evil pictures on the walls of his dormitory room. One day his mother came to visit him. She saw the evil pictures but said nothing. Instead she bought and sent to him the loveliest picture of Jesus that she could find. When she came back to visit him later, she saw only the picture of the Savior on the wall. "You know, Mother," he said, "I found the old, bad pictures would not go with this one. I had to take them down."

Questions About Overcoming Temptation

1. Does God tempt us? James 1:13.
2. What is Jesus doing for us now? Romans 8:34. Look up "interceding" in a dictionary.

3. How is the Word of God like a sword? Matthew 4:10, 11.
4. Someone has said, "You can't keep the birds from flying over your head, but you can keep them from building a nest in your hair." How does this apply to temptation?
5. Do Christians ever get to the place that they are no longer tempted? 1 Corinthians 10:12.
6. Is it a sin to be tempted? Matthew 4:1.
7. Are temptations good for us? James 1:2, 3.
8. Is it possible for the Christian to live a life of victory over sin? 1 John 5:4, 5.
9. How is the devil like an angel of light? 2 Corinthians 11:14.
10. How does Scripture memorization help us to live a victorious life? Psalm 119:11.

Reviewing the Lesson
   Bible Advice for Overcoming Temptation

1. I have hidden your _____ in my _____ that I might not _____ against you. Psalm 119:11.

2. _____ and _____ so that you will not fall into temptation. The spirit is _____, but the _____ is weak. Matthew 26:41.

3. Finally, be _____ in the _____ and in his mighty _____. Ephesians 6:10.

4. Put on the full _____ of _____ so that you can take your stand against the devil's _____. Ephesians 6:11.

5. But thanks be to God! He gives us the _____ through our _____ _____ _____. 1 Corinthians 15:57.

96

6. For everyone _____ _____ _____ has overcome the world. The is the victory that has overcome the world, even our _____. 1 John 5:4.

7. Who is it that overcomes the world? Only he who believes that _____ is the _____ _____ _____. 1 John 5:5.

8. Resist the devil, and he will _____ _____ _____. James 4:7.

Memory Verse

No temptation has seized you except what is common to man. And God is faithful; he will not let you be tempted beyond what you can bear. But when you are tempted, he will also provide a way out so that you can stand up under it. 1 Corinthians 10:13.

Play It Safe

A rich man once wanted to hire a new coach driver. He advertised, and a day was set for the trial run. Three men applied for the job. Each man was to prove his skill by driving a horse-drawn coach down a dangerous mountain road. The rich man and many others gathered below to watch.

The first man came down the mountainside in a cloud of dust, skillfully sweeping around the dangerous curve. He had come quite near to the edge of the road.

The next driver would need to do better. He also came rapidly down the mountain, coming even nearer the edge than the first driver.

The people held their breath. What chance had the last driver to make a better showing? If he tried to drive closer to the edge he would surely tumble over the cliff to destruction below.

The third driver began his trip down the mountain. What was wrong? Why did the coach move so slowly? The third driver

drove the horses carefully, staying as close to the mountain as he could. He took no chances. When he arrived at the bottom, the rich man said, "You are hired. You are the man I want to ride with."

People who try to live as near to sin as they can without sinning are very foolish. Christians should live as close to Jesus as possible.

Day by Day with Jesus

First Day. Three Enemies of the Christian Life.
Read Matthew 13:3-9, 18-23.

In the *Parable of the Sower* Jesus gives three reasons why people fail in Christian living. In the first case, the devil takes the Word away. In the next there are no roots; and in the third, things crowd out the Word. The three enemies of the soul are *the devil, self,* and *the world.* Temptation comes through each of these three. We cannot trust any of them to lead us to a strong Christian life.

The secret of victory is to recognize the enemy. The fall of Troy was described by Homer, a Greek poet. The Greeks had been trying to take the city of Troy for ten years with no success. Finally, they built a huge wooden horse, filled it with soldiers, and left it outside the city walls. The armies sailed away. The people of Troy did not recognize the horse as an enemy. They went out to look at it. At last they took it into the city. That night the Greeks hidden inside the horse got out and opened the gates of the city. The Greek armies returned, invaded the city, burned it to the ground and killed the people.

Second Day. Why Peter Failed.
Read Matthew 26:37-44.

In Lesson 2 we studied Peter's failure. Think again about Peter and what happened in his life. Here are six steps that led him to give in to temptation.

1. He was sure of himself. He boasted he would not forsake Jesus.
2. He did not pray. Jesus had told him, "Watch and pray."
3. He tried to get the victory in his own strength. He took a sword and cut off a man's ear to protect Jesus.
4. He followed afar off.
5. He got into bad company. He warmed himself at the enemy's fire.
6. He finally denied his Lord. For the whole story, read Matthew 26:31-75.

99

Third Day. Playing with Sin.

Read Genesis 3:1-6.

Eve played with the idea Satan suggested. As she looked at the fruit, she admired it. It looked good! Certainly no harm could come in handling it. So she took it. Soon she tasted, and then she ate of it.

No person is strong enough to play with sin. Sometimes young people read bad books and magazines, listen to evil radio programs, or watch immoral TV shows on the sly. They think that no harm can come from simply reading, listening, or watching. But they are mistaken. Playing with sin usually results in sin.

One time an alcoholic reformed, signed a pledge, and seemed to stop drinking. But when he drove to town he continued to park his car in front of the tavern. Soon he was back in the old habit!

Fourth Day. God Is Faithful.

Read 1 Corinthians 10:13.

God is able to save. God is also able to keep. We are often unfaithful to God, but God never fails us. In speaking of his sheep Jesus said, "My Father, who has given them to me, is greater than all; no one can snatch them out of my Father's hand" (John 10:29). As long as we are in the Father's hand we are safe. The trouble comes when we wander away from the Father's care.

Luke 15:4-7. Away from the Father's protection anything can happen.

The psalmist said, "He will cover you with his feathers, and under his wings you will find refuge" (Psalm 91:4).

Have you ever watched a mother hen and her chicks? During times of danger, the hen gives an alarm signal and all the chicks run under her wings to safety. Jesus said that he longs to protect his people as a hen does her chicks.

Fifth Day. The Holy Spirit Is Powerful.

Read Acts 1:8, 4:33.

The Holy Spirit is God. When the Holy Spirit lives in us the power of God is at work in our lives.

A striking example of how the Holy Spirit gives power for victory is found in Peter. The second day of this lesson we studied the steps in his downfall. Peter meant to do right but he lacked power to do it. It was as Jesus had said to him in the garden, "The spirit [Peter's spirit] is willing, but the body is weak" (Matthew 26:41).

On the Day of Pentecost the Holy Spirit came to live in Peter. He was now a man of victory. Nothing on earth could stop him. He became a bold preacher. He was not afraid of those who threatened him. He lived a holy life in the power of the Spirit.

We need not live defeated lives. We have the power of the Spirit. We receive the Holy Spirit by asking God for the Spirit, and by believing that the Spirit has been given to us.

Sixth Day. We Are More Than Conquerors.
Read Romans 8:37; Acts 16:25.
There are three ways to meet temptation:
1. We can be less than conquerors.
2. We can be conquerors.
3. We can be more than conquerors.
Can you decide what the following people were?

A schoolmate accused George, who claimed to be a Christian, of taking his pen. George hotly denied it. Then there were bitter words. The argument continued until the boy struck George, who became angry and struck back. Was George a conqueror, less than a conqueror, or more than a conqueror?

Mr. Jones, a Christian, bought a bushel of apples at the fruit market. Two days later, while canning the apples, his wife discovered that the ones in the bottom of the basket were spoiled. When Mr. Jones took the basket of apples back, the merchant declared that the apples were good when sold and would do nothing about it. Mr. Jones did not argue with the merchant but quietly decided that he would never do business with him again.

Peter Miller lived at Ephrata, Pennsylvania, during the Revolutionary War. Michael Wittman hated Miller and once spit in his face. Miller, being a Christian, did not strike back. Later Wittman was arrested as a Tory, found guilty, and was sentenced to be hanged. When Miller heard this, he went to George Washington and asked for Wittman's pardon. It was granted. Miller then walked many miles with the pardon, arriving at the place of the execution just in time to save his enemy.

Seventh Day. Victory Verses.
Read Isaiah 41:10.

The Word of God is the Christian's sword. We must memorize many Bible verses, to have them ready in time of temptation. When Jesus was tempted by Satan, he replied by quoting Bible verses. He did not need to look them up in a concordance first (of course, he had no concordance). He knew them by memory.

The Mennonite Publishing House has a tract called *Victory Verses*, which lists fifty helpful verses to memorize.

Be sure to learn the memory verses suggested in each lesson of this course.

The Bible on the table or even in the hand is not enough. It must be in the heart.

Working for Jesus
We do not work for Jesus to save ourselves. We work for him because we love him. The Lord will reward us if we are faithful day by day. Project 12 on page 140 is a good one to practice continually.

How to Walk with Jesus

Many Have Walked with Jesus

One of the best things to be said of any person was said of Enoch: "Enoch walked with God" (Genesis 5:24).

Since that time, many persons have walked with God. The Bible says that Noah walked "with God" and that David walked "before God." In New Testament times certain people were said to "follow" Jesus. Followers of Jesus were also called "disciples." A disciple is one who believes and practices the teachings of another. A Christian disciple is one who loves Jesus and obeys His teachings.

It is helpful to read the biographies of great Christians of the past. The New Testament has several. Your church library likely contains good biographies of more recent Christians.

One interesting book is *Martyrs Mirror*, written by van Braght. This is a large book. It tells of Christian martyrs from the time of Christ to 1660. In the time of Nero, Christians were dressed in skins of beasts and torn to pieces by dogs or other wild animals. Some were fastened alive on crosses; others were tied to stakes, covered with wax, and burned alive. To walk with Jesus— to be one of his disciples—was risky. Even today Christian people sometimes must die for their faith.

Read all the Christian biographies that you can. Read about *Martin Luther, David Livingstone, Ann of Ava, Grenfell of Labrador*. Read about *George Washington Carver*, the Christian Negro scientist, who discovered so many uses for the peanut that he is often called the "Peanut Man." Read how *Daniel Kauffman*, a leader in the Mennonite Church for fifty years, gave up politics to follow Christ. Read the story of *Fanny Crosby*, the blind hymn writer who believed her blindness was a blessing. Read about *Clayton Kratz* in the book, *When Apples Are Ripe*. Clayton disappeared in Russia while on a relief assignment following World War I.

Why read about all these people? Because our own faith is strengthened as we realize that we are part of a mighty army of men and women who have lived and suffered and walked with Christ.

Learning About Walking with Jesus
1. *Walking in Love.* Ephesians 5:2.

The most important thing in the Christian life is love. Henry Drummond wrote a little book on 1 Corinthians 13. In this he calls love *The Greatest Thing in the World.* No matter how much faith we have in Jesus, no matter how much work we do for him, if we do not have love in our hearts, we are not walking with Jesus. Everything we do must be done in love.

2. *Walking as a Faithful Servant.* Matthew 25:14, 19.

God is the owner of all things. We are only stewards. A steward is one who is placed in charge of another's possessions. A steward takes care of things according to the wishes of the owner. God has given us many things to watch over.

Our bodies, minds, abilities, time, money, personalities, and possessions all belong to God. They must be used to God's glory. Someday we will have to report to God on how we used them.

3. *Walking as a Lonely Pilgrim.* 1 Peter 2:11.

James R. Graham in his booklet, *Strangers and Pilgrims*, wrote: "The quiet little Chinese laundryman in your town is the best illustration we know of, of the pilgrim and stranger. Regardless of how many years he has been there, the chances are he has never become naturalized, and therefore has never voted or been conscripted for military service. He keeps the laws and pays his debts and lives in all decency and propriety. But he is always a foreigner, an unabsorbed stranger. He admits it, and has the firm intent of returning one day to China."

The Christian must often walk alone. The crowds are found on the broad way that leads to destruction. There are few walking on the way that leads to heaven. The Christian lives a *separated* life, not separated from people but from their evil ways. To understand the meaning of separation, John C. Wenger's book, *Separated unto God*, is very helpful. This book shows how the Christian should be different from the non-Christians in speech, recreation, dress, courtship and marriage, business, the care of the body, and the like.

4. *Walking as a Witness.* Acts 1:8.
The Lord wants all of his followers to be witnesses. A witness is a person who saw something happen. A witness can give a first-hand account of what occurred. A Christian witness tells others about his or her experience with Jesus. Before one has had an experience with Jesus, however, a person cannot witness, for one has nothing to tell. After a person becomes a Christian one will feel like the apostles when they said in Acts 4:20, "We cannot help speaking about what we have seen and heard."
We need to live a good life. But that is not enough. We need also to speak to others about Christ.
Dr. John Oliver Nelson says that there are five classes of Christians:
a. The strong, silent type, who say they just "live their faith."
b. Those who make remarks about their religion, such as saying they have been to church or that they read their Bibles.
c. The "Won't you attend?" type, who invite people to come to church services.
d. Those who talk publicly. They speak to the crowd but do not have courage to speak to the individual.
e. Those who share their personal faith with others personally.
In which class are you?

5. *Walking with Jesus in Daily Work.* Exodus 20:9; 2 Thessalonians 3:10.
Who is in full-time Christian service? Often people have the mistaken idea that only ministers or missionaries are in "full-time

service." But every Christian should be working full time for the Lord. Work is not a curse. It is a blessing. It is not a result of Adam's sin. Adam and Eve were given work to do in the Garden of Eden before they sinned. We should think of our work as a sacred calling from God. Jesus spent many of his thirty years working in Joseph's carpenter shop. We are sure he was doing the will of God there. His work was sacred and holy.

We should be certain, however, that we are doing the work God wants us to do. First ask God, "Lord, what do you want me to do?" God has a purpose for every person's life, and it is up to each Christian to find that purpose.

6. *Walking with Jesus in Wholesome Recreation.* Mark 6:31.

Everyone needs recreation. But we do not live to play. Rather, we play so that we can live better. Jesus realized that he and his disciples needed a change if they were to stay well in mind and body. There are many kinds of amusements and recreations—some good and some bad. Keep these things in mind:
   a. Avoid recreation which takes you into bad company.
   b. Do not become a slave to any game or amusement.
   c. Avoid expensive forms of recreation.
   d. Amusements which spoil your desire to worship God are not for the Christian.
   e. Recreation which leaves you tired and run down has really not "re-created" you.
   f. Sunday is a day for worship and rest.
   g. Avoid amusements which merely "kill time."
   h. Do nothing you would not want to be doing when Jesus returns.

7. *Walking with Jesus in Happy Family Living.* Ephesians 6:1-4.

Happy homes are not an accident. They are planned. Many young people just drift into marriage. They take more time in choosing an automobile than they do in choosing a life companion. Courtship is a serious time. There can be no truly happy homes unless it is built upon love, purity, unselfishness, and

106

prayer. Christ must have first place in the home.

The happy home is a place where children obey parents, parents train children, husbands love wives, and wives respect husbands.

Someone has said, "A person may succeed in the world, but if one fails at home, one is a failure. One may fail in the world, but if one succeeds at home, one is a success." By the grace of God we can succeed at home!

8. *Walking with Jesus in Sickness and Death.* James 5:14, 15; Psalm 23:4.

Unpleasant experiences will come even to Christians. The Lord does not keep us from sickness nor death, but gives us strength to face these things. Sometimes God heals those who are sick. In James 5:13-16 we read about the ordinance of anointing with oil. This is God's plan for healing the sick:

a. The sick person calls for the ministers.

b. The ministers anoint the sick person.

c. The ministers pray for the person.

d. Sins are confessed.

e. God forgives the sins and heals the body.

It is not God's will that every sick person should become well. If this were so, people would never die. As long as we are in this world, we have bodies that get sick. After the resurrection, our bodies will not become sick nor die.

Young people are often afraid to die. Death for the Christian is simply passing through a door into the presence of Christ. Death is not the end. It is the beginning of a wonderful new life!

Questions About Walking with Jesus

1. Can one be saved without walking with Jesus? John 15:6; Luke 9:23.

2. Are Christians promised an easy life? 2 Timothy 3:12.

3. What is the most important commandment? Matthew 22:36-38.

4. What kind of giver does the Lord appreciate? 2 Corinthians 9:7.

5. Can you name some Bible characters who walked alone with God? Hebrews 11:24-27.
6. Were the apostles the only witnesses in the early church? Compare Acts 8:1 (last part) with verse 4.
7. Is it possible to walk with Jesus every day of the week? Acts 18:1-4.
8. Is it out of place to have prayer at a social gathering? 1 Thessalonians 5:17, 18.
9. Should Christians ever get a divorce? Matthew 19:3-6.
10. Is sickness proof that a Christian is suffering from unconfessed sin? John 9:1-3.

Reviewing the Lesson
Cross out the things a Christian should *not* do:
1. Read a good book of Christian biography.
2. Pray for a forgiving spirit.
3. Love a person who is snobbish and proud.
4. Spend money for tobacco.
5. Take good care of property.
6. Try to follow the crowd.
7. Tell others about living for Christ.
8. Think of daily work as something holy.
9. Avoid amusements which merely "kill time."
10. Look forward to life after death.

Memory Verse
Then he said to them: "If anyone would come after me, he must deny himself and take up his cross daily and follow me. Luke 9:23.

Day by Day with Jesus
First Day. Faithfulness.
Read Genesis 45:3-15.
God expects us to take care of the bodies, time, and possessions God has given us. We are to put them to good use. Someday we will need to give an account of our stewardship.

God's word to us is, "Be faithful, even to the point of death, and I will give you the crown of life."

Joseph was a faithful person. As a boy he was faithful to his father. As a slave he was faithful to his master. In time of temptation he was faithful to God. In prison he was faithful to the keeper. As a ruler of Egypt he was faithful to his task. He was faithful in small things; this fitted him for greater responsibility.

Ask the Lord to help you to be faithful.

Second Day. Boldness.

Read Acts 4:8-21.

Peter and John were bold because they knew God was with them. With God all things are possible. God and you can do anything. A flea was once riding on an elephant's ear. As they crossed a bridge the flea said, "Did you notice how *we* made that bridge shake?"

When God spoke to Moses from the burning bush and asked him to go to Pharaoh, Moses said, "Who am I that I should go to Pharaoh?" God replied, "I will be with you." And God was. We do not read that Moses trembled before Pharaoh. When he was once convinced that God was with him, he was afraid of nothing.

Are we ashamed of Jesus? Are we ashamed to let others know that we are Christians? When the Holy Spirit comes into our lives, we receive power to witness for our Lord.

Third Day. Purity.

Read 1 Corinthians 6:15-20.

Our bodies are temples of God. They must be kept clean. God will not live in a dirty place. He is pure and holy. To be sure, God wants us to keep our bodies washed and free from grease and dirt. But that is not what the Bible means here. It is *sin* that makes one's body unfit to be a temple of the Holy Spirit.

Purity begins in the mind. As a weed in the garden, if allowed to grow, will choke out the good vegetables, so an impure thought in the mind, if let go, will crowd out good thoughts. It is dangerous to read bad books and magazines, to listen to or tell off-color stories, or to do impure daydreaming. Wrong thinking results in wrong living.

Because smoking and drinking weaken the body, they are sinful. Anything that tears down the body and ruins it is wrong.

What reason does God give for being holy and pure in 1 Peter 1:16? Be holy because ____ _____ _____.

Fourth Day. Obedience.

Read John 15:10-14.

To walk with Jesus means to obey him. What does Jesus say in John 14:15? If you love me, you will _____ what I

_____.

Many years ago there was a terrible fire in Hartford, Connecticut. A father rushed his children to a place of safety only to discover that his small boy was missing. Finally, after a long search, he gave up hope and returned to his car. There he found the little boy sitting, waiting for him. The little fellow explained, "You always taught me to go to the car if I ever got lost from you."

Jesus loves us and will ask us to do only that which is for our good. Pray that the Lord will give you a heart of willingness to obey.

Fifth Day. Humility.

Read Psalm 23.

The Lord is shepherd to those who want to be led. We must be humble enough to admit that we do not know the way, that we need someone to guide us.

On April 10, 1912, the *Titanic*, the largest ship the world had ever known, sailed from Southampton on her first voyage across the Atlantic. Everyone thought the *Titanic* was unsinkable. It had double bottoms and sixteen watertight compartments. It was described as a gigantic lifeboat. The crew was warned of icebergs in the area, but even Captain Smith paid little attention to the warnings. After all, the *Titanic* was unsinkable! At 11:40 in the night the *Titanic* struck an iceberg. A 300-foot slash was made in the bottom of the ship. At first no one worried. The *Titanic* was unsinkable! But the *Titanic* did sink—and with her, more than 1,500 persons. Only 704 persons were saved.

People who are proud, who do not feel the need of God, will come to a dreadful end. Pray for humility.

Sixth Day. Trust.

Read Daniel 6:10-23.

"And when Daniel was lifted from the den, no wound was found on him, because he had trusted in his God."

Daniel could have worried all night while in the lions' den. Many people worry about much less. Worry is not only useless; it is actually harmful. People can and do worry themselves sick.

The janitor of a big city church found a crumpled piece of note paper on the same bench every week. After some time he opened one of the papers to find the words: "Clara—ill; Lester—job; rent." Each week the janitor found the paper wads and read the words. Then he began watching for the person who left them there. It was a middle-aged woman. She always came alone.

The janitor finally told the pastor, who one day spoke to the woman, showing her some of the crumpled bits of paper. She explained, "Some time ago I saw a sign among advertising posters in a streetcar. It said, 'Take your troubles to church with you.' My troubles are written on those pieces of paper. I write them down during the week, bring them here on Sunday mornings—and leave them. God takes care of them."

Can you claim this Bible promise? Cast all your _____ on him because he _____ _____ _____. 1 Peter 5:7.

Seventh Day. Happiness.

Read Acts 16:19-25.

Happiness does not depend on our surroundings. Can you

111

imagine anyone sitting in prison, feet in stocks, back bleeding, and still able to sing? Happiness is an inner experience. True happiness is possible only when the peace and love of God fill the heart. Here are some rules for happiness:

1. Let Jesus take your burden of sin away.
2. Live for others instead of self.
3. Be satisfied with what you have.
4. Work hard.
5. Walk with Jesus every day.

"Happiness is neither within us only, nor without us; it is the union of ourselves with God."—Pascal.

Working for Jesus

People say, "I would do this or that—if I had time." If we wait until we "have time" we will never do anything. We must "take" time. We generally find time to do the things we consider important. We find time to do the things we want to do. Take time to do projects 2 or 17 on page 140 this week.

How to Study the Bible

Thank God for the Bible

The person without a Bible is like a person without a light on a dark night or like a sailor on a stormy sea without a compass. Have you ever tried to imagine what the world would be like without the Bible?

We should be thankful that we live in a land where Bible-reading is encouraged and where education is free so that all can learn to read. Before printing was invented, Bibles were expensive. A scribe had to work about ten months to make one copy. It took about a year's wages to buy a Bible. If that were true today, a Bible would cost many thousands of dollars.

The Bible has been precious to Christians of all ages. The British and Foreign Bible Society has in its collection a Welsh Bible published in 1799. On the front page are written these words, "Mary Jones, the true owner of this Bible. Bought in the year 1800. Aged 16. For more than six years this poor peasant girl saved her money to buy a copy of the Bible. It was twenty-five miles from her village to the place where the Bibles were for sale. She walked the entire distance to secure the longed-for Book."

If you were to spend the rest of your life on a lonely island and could take only one book along, what would you take? If you were to sell the Bible you have, knowing that you could never get another one, how much would you ask for it?

When the explorer Stanley started across the continent of Africa, he had seventy-three books along in three packs weighing 180 pounds. After traveling 300 miles, he was forced to throw away some of his books because it was too difficult for his servants to carry them. As he continued he had to get rid of more of his library, until at last he had only one book left—the Bible.

Most of us know that the Bible is important. We realize that it is impossible for us to grow in the Christian life without reading it. But many people find the Bible a dry, uninteresting book. They find it hard to understand. They read it from a sense of duty. They do not enjoy reading it. They read it because they feel they should. "A chapter a day keeps the conscience away."

On the other hand there are people who enjoy the Bible. They are like David. The Bible to him was "more precious than gold, than much pure gold; they are sweeter than honey . . . from the comb" (Psalm 19:10). They feel they cannot live without the Bible. They must have it. They are like William McPherson of Kansas City.

A Lover of the Bible

This is a picture of William McPherson, the blind, handless man of Kansas City, Missouri, who learned to read the Bible in a strange way. On June 21, 1906, while working in a stone quarry, an unexpected blast blew him about twenty feet away, resulting in the loss of his eyes and hands. After much effort and prayer, he learned to read with his tongue. The Bible shown here is printed in Moon type used by the blind, and consists of 57 volumes.

How to Enjoy Bible Study
1. Know the Author.
We will not enjoy Bible reading until we learn to know the Author, until we are born again, until we are saved.

D. L. Moody wrote inside the cover of one of his Bibles, "Either this book will keep you from sin, or sin will keep you from this book." People who have never had their sins forgiven do not like to read the Bible. It makes them feel uncomfortable.

A girl was reading a book while riding a train. She tried to become interested in the book but found it quite dry. After a while a fine-looking young man took the seat beside her. She became acquainted with him and was impressed with the young man's character. During the conversation she learned that he was the author of the book she had been trying to read. When the man got off the train, she again turned to her book. Now it was not hard to read, because she had met the author.

2. Learn the Rules.
People who do not understand the rules of a game find it boring to watch. They also find it boring to try to play.

One man became discouraged in trying to read the New Testament because he said it "repeated itself." He did not know that the Bible is a collection of sixty-six books written by many different writers. He did not understand that Matthew, Mark, Luke, and John each wrote a separate story of the life of Christ.

To enjoy reading the Bible we need to understand that:

a. The Bible was written to tell us of the plan of salvation.

b. The Bible is God's message to us.

c. The central person in the Bible is Jesus Christ.

d. Whole paragraphs, chapters, and books must be read to understand the single verses.

e. One part of the Bible often explains another part.

f. The New Testament builds upon the Old Testament.

To enjoy Bible study we should learn to know the names and order of all its sixty-six books. We should use the Bible so much that we are as well acquainted with the chapters and verses as we are with the streets and houses of friends in our city. We feel at home in our city because we travel its streets and visit its homes and stores. We feel at home in our Bible by visiting its books, chapters, and verses.

3. *Own the Proper Tools.*

First of all we should own a good *Bible*, one that has good paper and readable print. It should have references, arranged so that we can refer to other verses in the Bible that explain the verse we are studying. A good Bible will have maps.

A *dictionary* is a necessary tool. The Bible is made up of words. The words must be understood if the Bible is to be enjoyed.

Every Christian should own a *Bible dictionary*. This tool will tell of persons, places, and things mentioned in the Bible.

Another necessary book is a *Bible concordance*. A concordance lists all words used in the Bible and tells where they are found. Other *versions* or *translations* of the Bible are also helpful.

We need good tools to understand the Bible. A mechanic, plumber, or carpenter would not think of working without tools. For a few dollars we can buy these basic tools for Bible study, which we will use for life.

4. *Read Prayerfully.*

We should always come to the Bible with a prayer. We should ask God to teach us the truth of the Word through the Holy Spirit. It is a mistake to read the Bible so that we can argue about it or only to teach it. God has a message for *our* souls. We must ask God to teach us that message. Our eyes are often blind to the truth. We should pray:

> Open my eyes, that I may see
> Glimpses of truth Thou hast for me;

Place in my hands the wonderful key
That shall unclasp, and set me free.
Silently now I wait for Thee,
Ready, my God, Thy will to see;
Open my eyes, illumine me,
Spirit divine!—Clara H. Scott

5. *Read Every Day.*

Everyone should have a certain time each day to read the Bible. For some, morning is the best time; for others, evening. If we do not have a regular time to read, we are apt to forget or neglect it. Why should we not have a regular time to feed our souls? We eat every day. We sleep every night. We wash our faces every morning. We dare not be too busy or too lazy for regular Bible reading.

God taught the children of Israel to gather the manna from heaven every day. We must gather "manna" from God's Word each day if we are to grow spiritually.

6. *Look for a Blessing.*

Have you ever read a page and then were unable to tell what you read? This can be overcome by looking for something as you read. Never leave your private devotions until you have found something which you can take along with you for the day. Here are some things to watch for as you read:

An example to be followed
A truth to be learned
A teaching to be received
A promise to be claimed
A command to be obeyed
A warning to be heeded
An error to be avoided
A prayer to be prayed
A condition to be met
An application to be tried
A response to be made

7. Read and Reread.

An old Latin proverb says, "Read and read; something will be remembered." We cannot get everything from a chapter by reading it once. Each time we read it we see something new.

One of the great Bible teachers was G. Campbell Morgan. He said that he read the book of Exodus through forty times—at one sitting each time—before he put his pencil to paper for his notes on it. George Müller read the Bible through four times a year, more than one hundred times in all. George Lapp, Mennonite missionary to India, read the Bible fifty-one times the last fifty years of his life. One year he read it twice.

Reading is not enough. We must also think. Meditation is another word for thinking. We live in such a fast world that we scarcely have time to meditate. We should read and then think about what we have read.

8. Read to Obey.

It is easier to understand the Bible than to obey its commands. But those who obey it understand it best. In John 7:17 we are told, "If any one chooses to do God's will, he will find out whether my teaching comes from God." We must obey if we are to know the Word of God.

Coming out of a church one Sunday evening a man was stopped by a friend, who inquired with a smile, "Is the sermon done?"

"No," came the reply; "it is preached, but it has yet to be done."

Many people read the Bible like the man described in James 1:22-24. This man looked into the mirror of God's Word and saw that he had a dirty face, but went his way and completely forgot about it.

Read the story Jesus told about people who hear his sayings, in Matthew 7:24-29.

9. Memorize.

Bible passages you memorize are yours. They cannot be

taken away from you. D. L. Moody said, "Learn at least one verse of Scripture each day. Verses committed to memory will be wonderfully useful in your daily life."

Henry H. Halley was called the "Bible Memory Wizard." It is estimated that he memorized one fourth of the Bible. There was a time when he could recite the Scriptures for twenty-six hours without repeating himself. Mr. Halley claimed he had a very ordinary memory. He learned his verses through hard work, spending two or three hours a day for ten years. Did he enjoy doing it? Yes, indeed! He said it never became a chore. He called it an "adventure." He was thirty-nine years old when he began.

Anyone can memorize the Bible, but it takes work. Levi Wenger, an Ohio man, memorized the Book of John, the Book of Romans, the Sermon on the Mount, fifty of the Psalms, and other passages, after he was sixty years old. He said that memorizing left him tired. It was hard work. But he also said that it changed his life and was a real blessing.

Here are some suggestions for memorizing:

a. Learn paragraphs or chapters. It is usually better to learn something as a whole rather than in parts.

b. Try to understand the meaning of the verse you are learning.

c. Repeat and repeat. Say it over and over. Say it aloud. By reading aloud, you hear as well as see.

d. Write the verses from memory. This is a good way to help you remember them.

e. "Overlearn" the materials. The way to remember anything is to keep going over it even after you think you know it. Unless material is "overlearned," experiments show that about sixty per cent is forgotten within twenty-four hours.

f. Keep reviewing. Mr. Wenger, mentioned above, said he had to spend one hour a day reviewing, just to keep what he had learned.

10. *Have a plan.* Unless one has a plan one will neglect Bible reading. Here are several suggestions:

a. Study the Sunday school lesson every day. Read the daily Bible readings listed. Part of the lesson can be read each day.

b. Read the Bible through. By reading three chapters every weekday and five on Sundays you can read the whole Bible in a year. In general, we should read the New Testament more often than the Old Testament, because it is more important for the Christian. If we would read three chapters in each Testament each day, in a year's time we could read the Old Testament through once and the New Testament three or four times.

c. Use a daily Bible reading chart. It is helpful to have a chart which has a square for each chapter in the Bible. As chapters are read they may be marked. This way the Bible need not be read in the exact order. Write to the American Bible Society, 1865 Broadway, New York, N.Y. 10023 for a folder listing daily Bible reading for each day of the year.

d. Have a book that asks questions or discusses each chapter of the Bible. The chapter in the Bible may be read first, then the book may be used.

Many good daily devotional guides are available. See the Mennonite Publishing House catalog or inquire from the nearest Provident bookstore for suggestions.

e. Build your own notebook. Jot down your comments, questions, and thoughts on each chapter.

Questions About Enjoying the Bible
1. Why has God given us the Bible?
2. Why is the Bible an uninteresting book to many people?
3. How do you account for the fact that some Christians seldom read the Bible?
4. Can a person be a good Christian without reading the Bible regularly?
5. What three reference books should every Christian own?
6. Of what value is another translation in making Bible study enjoyable?
7. Is marking the Bible a helpful habit?
8. How is the Bible different from other books?

9. What things should one look for when reading the Bible?
10. What rules are helpful in memorizing the Bible?

Reviewing the Lesson
True or False?

F 1. It is impossible for a young person to become interested in reading the Bible.

T 2. Every strong Christian is a regular Bible reader.

T 3. The Holy Spirit helps us to understand the Bible.

T 4. Jesus Christ is the main character in the Bible.

T 5. One part of the Bible explains another part.

F 6. The New Testament often does not agree with the Old Testament.

T 7. The words in the Bible must be understood if the Bible is to be enjoyed.

T 8. Every Christian should own a Bible dictionary.

T 9. When we read the Bible we should be looking for something for our souls.

T 10. The Bible should be read every day.

F 11. We should not obey the Bible until we fully understand it.

F 12. Only very good students can memorize Scripture.

F 13. It is not very important to have a plan for Bible study.

T 14. One good plan is to study the Sunday school lesson.

F 15. All that the Bible teaches about the Savior is found in the New Testament.

F 16. One should not spend too much time on a certain verse; one should hurry on to the next to cover more material.

Memory Verse
But his delight is in the law of the Lord, and on his law he meditates day and night. Psalm 1:2.

Day by Day with Jesus
First Day. Fellowship with God.
Read 1 Kings 19:4-8.
Adam and Eve enjoyed fellowship with God each day in the

beginning. After they sinned, they were afraid of God and no longer enjoyed hearing God speak. When our sins are taken away by the blood of Christ, we again enjoy hearing the voice of God through the Bible. In Bible reading God talks to us. In prayer we talk to God. Fellowship is a two-way process. We listen to God speak. We say *yes* to God. We say *Amen,* meaning "let it be so."

Elijah was discouraged. He was afraid the wicked queen was going to kill him. He ran away to the woods. Then God came and encouraged him and he was strengthened. God gave him food to eat. When we are discouraged, we will find strength to go on as we read the promises of God in the Bible.

Second Day. The Christian's Library.

Read 1 Timothy 4:13.

Paul was a great reader. He encouraged Timothy and others to read. He loved his library.

The Bible is the most important book in the library and should be used the most. But there are many other helpful books which help us to understand, use, and teach the Bible.

We have mentioned that the Christian's library should contain a dictionary, a Bible dictionary, and a Bible concordance. Besides this, there are many other good books you will want to add to your library from time to time. You will want Bible translations, commentaries, Christian biographies, a Bible atlas, books on the Christian life, and books on church history. But only the best books. Buy books you have examined. Buy books slowly and carefully. It is better to have a few good books than many poor ones.

Use the Mennonite Publishing House catalog for suggestions. Better still, visit one of our bookstores where you can examine books before buying. Ask Christian Bible students which books they consider helpful, and why.

Third Day. The Quiet Time.

Read Mark 1:35; Acts 10:9-16.

There is a time to be with people and there is a time to be alone with God. That is the way Jesus lived. It is the way he taught his followers to live. It is during the quiet time that we get strength for the busy times. Choose a place—a quiet place—where you can be comfortable and alone. Go to that place each day to read your Bible and pray. It will become a precious place to you. The Garden of Gethsemane on the Mount of Olives was one of Jesus' favorite places to pray. He was in the habit of going there. Luke 22:39.

George Washington Carver, the black scientist of the South, was a very busy man. During his lifetime, he discovered more than 300 uses for the common peanut. He was busy, but he took time to be alone with God. When he was asked how he discovered so many things about the peanut, he said, "God tells me the secrets. I get up every morning, winter and summer, at four. First I go into the woods and gather specimens and listen to what God has to say to me. After I have had my morning talk with God, I go to my laboratory and begin to carry out his wishes for the day."

Fourth Day. Discovering Bible Treasures.

Read Acts 8:26-39.

The man in the chariot was reading his Bible. He was trying to understand it. He was digging for the right answer. How thrilled he must have been when he discovered the meaning of what he was reading! It is always exciting when one finds something for oneself. Jesus promised a reward to all those who earnestly seek. He said, "Ask and it will be given to you; seek and you will find; knock and the door will be opened to you" (Matthew 7:7).

D. L. Moody once gave several days to the study of "grace." The more he studied, the more excited he became with what he found. When he had finished, he was so full of the subject that he rushed out on the street. Going up to the first man he met, he said: "Do you know anything about grace?"

"Grace who?" the man asked.

"The grace of God that brings salvation." And then Moody shared with the man the rich treasures he had dug out of God's Word.

Fifth Day. Sharing with Others.

Read Acts 4:13-21.

The more we share the Bible with others, the more we enjoy it ourselves. "It is more blessed (happy) to give than to receive." The more we give, the more we have.

The poor widow in the time of Elijah, who shared her last handful of meal with the prophet, never lacked. God saw to it that her meal barrel was never empty.

The boy who gave his lunch to Jesus still had plenty to eat; and, in addition, more than 5,000 were fed.

The farmer who sows a bag of seed gets back what was sowed, plus much more.

So it is in the spiritual life. If we share with others the precious truths which we discover in the Bible, both we and they will have plenty.

Find Luke 6:38 and fill in the missing words. _____,

and it will be _____ to you. A _____ _____,

_____ down, _____ together and _____ over,

will be poured into your lap.

Sixth Day. Studying the Sunday School Lesson.

Read 2 Timothy 2:15.

Everyone should study the Sunday school lesson, whether a teacher or not. God expects us all to study and eventually to become teachers. If we can read, we can study. If we can study, we can know. If we can know, we can tell others. When we tell others, we teach.

Here are several suggestions to follow in studying a Sunday school lesson:

1. Read the lesson from the Bible.
2. Look up all words you do not understand in a dictionary.
3. Find all places mentioned on a Bible map.
4. Study special names and places in a Bible dictionary.
5. Read the comments in the pupil book.

6. Read and study the daily readings.
7. Study the questions provided in the quarterly.

Seventh Day. How Much Do You Know About the Bible?
Read Psalm 1.

We must study the Bible if we would know it. We should be well acquainted with the great passages of the Bible, especially, and know where to find them. Use your Bible to fill in the blanks with these references: Psalm 23; Matthew 28:19, 20; Luke 10; 1 Corinthians 13; Matthew 6:9-13; Exodus 20; Luke 2; Luke 15; Genesis 1; Matthew 5-7.

1. The Sermon on the Mount __Matthew 5-7__
2. The Great Commission. __Matthew 28:19,20__
3. The Lost Son. __Luke 15__
4. The Good Samaritan. ~~Luke 2~~ __Luke 10__
5. The Love Chapter. __1 Corinthians 13__
6. The Ten Commandments. __Exodus 20__
7. The Christmas Story of the Shepherds. __Luke 2__
8. The Lord's Prayer. __Matthew 6:9-13__
9. The Shepherd's Psalm. __Psalm 23__
10. The Story of Creation. __Genesis 1__

Working for Jesus

The Christian never goes on a vacation from living as a Christian. As long as God allows us to live, God has work for us to do. Some Christians work hard at first, but after a time become lazy and indifferent. The Lord will reward us for our faithfulness. The Christian should be able to say, as Jesus did at the close of his earthly life, "I have brought you glory on earth by completing the work you gave me to do." (John 17:4).

The Story of Our Church

How the Mennonite Church Began

The church was started by Jesus in New Testament times. Since then, there has always been a church. But during these 2,000 years the church has often drifted away from Christ and become cold and indifferent. Sometimes it has wandered so far away from the truth that it could hardly be called the church of Christ.

Such was the case more than 450 years ago, when the Mennonite Church began. The main church in Europe at that time was the Roman Catholic Church, of which those who began the Mennonite Church were members. The Catholic Church of that day did not encourage its people to read the Bible. Latin was used in the worship services, and the people could not understand it. They did not know what the Bible taught. Only the educated, who had learned to read in Latin, Hebrew, or Greek, could know what the Bible said.

There were in Zurich, Switzerland, around the year 1520, several young persons who were educated and could read the Bible in the languages in which it was written. Among them was Conrad Grebel, who was a good Greek student, and Felix Manz. who was an especially good Hebrew scholar. As they read their Bibles they saw that the Roman Church was not teaching the truth.

1. The Bible teaches that salvation is a gift from God, received by faith. The Roman Church taught that to be saved one had to *do* certain things to earn salvation.

2. The Bible teaches that we can pray directly to God through Christ. The Roman Church told the people to confess their sins to the priest.

3. The Bible teaches that God alone is to be worshiped. The Roman Church encouraged prayer to Mary, the apostles, the martyrs, and angels.

4. The Bible teaches that baptism is a sign that sin has been washed away.

5. The Bible teaches that persons must believe before they can be baptized. The Roman Church baptized babies before they were old enough to understand and believe.

6. The Bible teaches that there are two places in the future world: heaven and hell. The Roman Church taught that there was a third place called "purgatory."

7. The Bible teaches that both the bread and the wine are to be served to believers in the communion service. The Roman Church did not serve the wine to the people.

8. The Bible teaches that the Christian should love all people. The Roman Church used force, and its members served in the army.

9. The Bible teaches that church and state must be kept separate, because the church is a fellowship of saints. The Roman Church was linked with earthly governments and participated in state affairs.

10. The Bible teaches that the Word of God alone is the authority for faith and life. The Roman Church claimed that its teachings and traditions were just as important as, or even more important than, Bible teaching.

One winter day in January, 1525, a group of these young Bible students met together near Zurich for study and prayer. They often met in such Bible meetings. The leaders were well educated and made good teachers. They knew the Bible and could explain it. These leaders and teachers often discussed these questions with a man by the name of Zwingli, who had left the Roman Catholic Church and had started a new church. But because Zwingli did not take a firm stand on all Bible teachings, they were not willing to belong to his church.

And so it was that on January 21, 1525, these students started a new church which later came to be known as the Mennonite Church.

Conrad Grebel, the leader of the group, baptized George Blaurock (Bluecoat), and Blaurock in turn baptized the others present.

In the beginning the new church was small. Because this group taught some things which were different, it was severely persecuted. Many early Mennonites died for their faith. But the movement continued in spite of the persecution. Soon there were groups of believers in South Germany and Austria. Farther north in the Netherlands, more churches were formed under the leadership of Menno Simons. There the movement spread rapidly, and congregations sprang up in North Germany, Prussia, and Poland. Later some of the people moved to Russia and started churches there.

Years later these European Mennonites came to America along with the other settlers. But it was not until 1683 that the first permanent Mennonite settlement was made at Germantown, Pennsylvania.

The Mennonite settlers came to America in four great waves. Between 1709 and 1754 from three to five thousand Swiss and German Mennonites came to eastern Pennsylvania. The second wave of settlers came to western Pennsylvania, Ohio, Indiana, Illinois, and Iowa, between 1815 and 1861, from Switzerland and Alsace. They came to America to escape military service and to find better homes. The other two waves of Mennonites came from Russia to the western states and Canada. After the first World War some of the Russian Mennonites found homes in Brazil and Paraguay. Through these movements and through our mission program we now have Mennonite churches on every continent of the world except Antarctica.

University Student Becomes First Mennonite Leader

Six years after Columbus discovered America, a baby boy was born in Zurich, Switzerland, named Conrad Grebel. Conrad's father was a wealthy iron merchant who was also important in government life. Coming from such a family, Conrad was naturally given the best of everything. He made friends with the leading families of Switzerland and studied in the best universities in Europe. He was a talented young man and had a promising future.

But he was not happy. Neither money nor education could bring peace of soul. During his university days he lived a loose, carefree life. He was not deeply religious. He was sick, unhappy, and discontented.

Conrad had an adventurous spirit. One summer when he was about twenty years old, he, together with some of his friends, climbed Pilatus, a 6,995-foot mountain of the Alps in central Switzerland.

At the age of twenty-three he fell in love with a girl named Barbara. He called her his "Whole World." But because she was not from an upper-class family like the Grebels, Conrad's family was against the match. Finally, however, they were married and had three children. Theophilus, Joshua, and Rachel.

It was under the preaching of the powerful Ulrich Zwingli that Conrad found Christ. Zwingli's preaching was different. He preached in the language of the people. He went through entire books of the Bible. He preached that salvation was to be found, not in fasting and certain religious ceremonies, but through faith in Christ. One man said that when Zwingli preached, it seemed that he held him by the hair of his head.

Conrad Grebel was converted and became a different person. He no longer complained about his health. He was now on fire for God. He was interested in Bible study and prayer. He wanted to know and to do the will of God. He did not keep this new-found joy to himself but threw himself into the work of teaching others. He went about preaching that the church must return to the New Testament pattern; that the church is made up of true believers who leave all to follow Christ. His message was not well received. Even Zwingli, his old friend, was not willing to carry the gospel that far, and he began to persecute Conrad.

Conrad Grebel's ministry was short. He lived only eighteen months after the events of 1525. At least nine of those months were spent in prison. He died at the age of twenty-eight of the plague. Had he lived longer he would no doubt have written many books and preached many sermons. His few years as a Christian were packed with fruitful activity. Had he not died of natural causes he might have been killed for his faith, as were his friends.

Felix Manz Dies for His Lord

One of the early Mennonite leaders was Felix Manz. He and his friends held regular Bible meetings at his mother's home in Zurich after the new church had been formed. Manz taught the life of love, that all believers should be baptized, and that the church and state should be separate. Because of his teachings, Felix and twenty of his friends were thrown into the "Witch Tower." A month later they escaped. Soon afterward they were again captured and put back into prison. This happened several times until finally Manz was sentenced to die.

At three o'clock in the afternoon on January 5, 1527, Manz was led past the fish market toward the river. As he went, he praised God with a loud voice. His mother stood on the other side of the river and encouraged her son to remain faithful.

Manz was taken out in a boat on the Limmat River which flows through the city of Zurich. He was bound hand and foot. A stick was pushed between his elbows and his knees to keep him from swimming. A state clergyman called to Manz, urging him to give up his faith and save his life. But Felix Manz remained faithful to the end. Just before his enemies dropped him into the water he cried out in Latin, "Into thy hands, O Lord, I commend my spirit."

How Our Church Was Named

The leaders of the new church in Switzerland, in 1525, did not choose the name *Mennonite* for themselves. They called themselves *Brethren*. Their enemies called them *Anabaptists*, which means *rebaptizers*. This was because they taught that a person should be baptized upon confession of faith in Christ, even though one had already been "baptized" as a baby. The name *Mennonite* comes from Menno Simons, a strong leader of the churches in Holland and North Germany. The term *Menist* was used about 1544 but was later changed to *Mennonite*. The name was carried from Holland into Germany and Switzerland, and finally to America.

Menno Simons was a Catholic priest for many years. He was a typical priest of his time, taking care of his church duties, but spending much of his time in card playing and drinking. His conversion was not a sudden one. It came after a long period of struggle. The struggle began in 1525, the very first year of his service as a priest. (This was the same year that the church began in Switzerland. But Menno knew nothing of the Brethren in Switzerland at that time. God was working in both places at once.)

Menno had doubts regarding the Catholic teaching on communion and baptism. He decided to seek help from the New Testament, a book he had read very little before this time. After years of study and prayer, he at last decided to leave the Roman Catholic Church. He was baptized in January, 1536, and soon afterwards was called to be an elder or bishop in the church.

For twenty-five years Menno Simons lived the life of a traveling evangelist and bishop. His life was often in danger as he worked in Holland and northwest Germany. A price of two thousand guilders was placed on his head, but he escaped his enemies, died a natural death in 1561, and was buried in his own garden.

Menno Simons was undoubtedly the greatest leader in the history of the Mennonite Church. In addition to his traveling and preaching, he wrote a great many books which were collected and published soon after his death. These books were written in Dutch and were later translated into German and English. The English collection, *The Complete Writings of Menno Simons* (Herald Press), has 1,090 pages.

Other Mennonite Groups

There are many different branches of Mennonites in the United States and Canada today, totaling more than 300,000 persons. Our group is called the Mennonite Church. There are more than 100,000 members in our church in the United States and Canada.

Study the *Mennonite Yearbook* to learn about the other

groups of Mennonites. The *Mennonite Yearbook* will also tell you about the committees, missions, and general work of our church.

Two Church Leaders

John F. Funk was a Mennonite leader in printing and publishing. In 1864 he began to publish a magazine called the *Herald of Truth*. Funk came to Chicago just before the Civil War to engage in the lumber business. He was interested in Sunday schools and worked with D. L. Moody for a time. He later moved to Elkhart, Indiana, where he set up the Mennonite Publishing Company. In 1908 the work was moved to Scottdale, Pennsyl-

John F. Funk

John S. Coffman

vania, and the Mennonite Publishing House was founded. John F. Funk lived to be almost ninety-five years old. Through his magazine Funk encouraged the church to start Sunday schools, missions, and evangelistic work. He no doubt did more for the Mennonite Church than any other man of his day.

John S. Coffman lived from 1848-1899. He is remembered as the first Mennonite evangelist. In a day when evangelistic preaching was uncommon in our church, Coffman went from congregation to congregation holding meetings, and winning persons to Christ. He was a deeply spiritual man and spent a great deal of time in prayer and fasting. In 1879 he moved to Elkhart, Indiana, where he worked with John F. Funk as assistant editor of the *Herald of Truth*. He was also interested in education and helped establish Elkhart Institute (now Goshen College) in 1895.

Questions About the Mennonite Church
Fill in the blanks.

1. _John S. Coffman_ a spiritual man of prayer who lived from 1848-1899, is best remembered for his evangelistic work.

2. The enemies of the early Mennonites called them _antibabtist_ because they believed that infants should be rebaptized when they became old enough to believe.

3. _Menno Simons_ was a Roman Catholic priest who, after a long struggle, became a Mennonite preacher and leader.

4. The early Mennonites in Switzerland called themselves _brethren_

5. Menno Simons went to the _New Testiment_ to find the answer to his doubts concerning communion and baptism.

6. _Felix Manz_ was an early Mennonite who was drowned in the Limmat River rather than give up his faith.

7. _Menno Simons_ was the man who began the Mennonite Church.

8. The Mennonite Church began in the country of _Switzerland_

9. The first Mennonite settlement in America began in
German Town , _Penn._____, in the year
_1683_

10. The early leaders of the Mennonite Church left the
_Roman Catholic_____ Church and started a
new church.

Reviewing the Lesson
True or False?

_F_ 1. Salvation is not something one can earn. It is a gift from
God received by faith in Christ.

_F_ 2. To have one's sins forgiven, they must be confessed to a
priest.

_T_ 3. Babies should not be baptized because they are not old
enough to understand and believe.

_T_ 4. The Bible teaches that Christians should love all people.

_F_ 5. The Bible teaches that one should pray to the Virgin Mary
and the Apostles.

_T_ 6. Conrad Grebel was converted under the preaching of Ulrich Zwingli.

_T_ 7. Many early Mennonites were killed for their faith.

_T_ 8. Many of the Mennonites came to America from Europe to
escape military service.

_F_ 9. Conrad Grebel lived before Columbus discovered America.

_F_ 10. Conrad Grebel was an uneducated man.

_T_ 11. Felix Manz went to his death praising God.

_T_ 12. For twenty-five years Menno Simons lived the life of a
traveling evangelist and bishop.

_T_ 14. The *Mennonite Yearbook* is a valuable help in understanding the Mennonite Church today.

_T_ 15. John F. Funk, an American Mennonite writer and printer,
published a magazine called the *Herald of Truth*.

Memory Verse

The boundary lines have fallen for me in pleasant places;
surely I have a delightful inheritance. Psalm 16:6.

Day by Day with Jesus
First Day. The Christian Way Is the Bible Way.

Read Acts 17:1-2.

The believers at Thessalonica did not go to the Bible to learn
the truth as those at Berea had done. The first Mennonites went
to the Bible for the answers to their questions. For persons like
Conrad Grebel and Menno Simons it made no difference what in-
dividuals, churches, or governments said. The important question
to them was, "What does the Bible teach?"

"No other people during the Reformation period knew the
contents of the Bible as did the Anabaptists," says C. Henry
Smith. They had a sincere desire to follow everything God taught
through the Bible.

Thank God for the ability to read and the privilege of owning
a Bible, that by the Spirit we can learn God's will for our lives.

Second Day. The Christian Way Is the Way of Suffering.

Read Hebrews 11:32-40.

Felix Manz was one of the first of many Mennonites who
died for the faith. In the first ten years over five thousand of the
Swiss Brethren (Mennonites) were killed. Before being executed
they were often tortured. They were hung up by their thumbs;
hot irons were put to their flesh; some of them were tied to wagon
wheels which were then driven down the street.

Are we willing to suffer a bit of ridicule for our faith? Can all
Christians expect some suffering? 2 Timothy 3:12.

Ask the Lord to give you strength to remain faithful even in
the face of persecution.

Third Day. We Must Obey God Whatever the Cost.

Read Acts 5:27-42.

Compare verses 29 and 42. Ulrich Zwingli's mistake was to

be more interested in following the decisions of the city council of Zurich than the teachings of the Bible. The Bible clearly teaches that the way in which the Roman Catholics held their mass (communion) was wrong. When the early Mennonites wanted Zwingli to do away with the mass, he refused. He knew that the city council was not ready to do so. So he said, "The council will decide concerning the mass."

At that Simon Stumpf cried out, "Master Ulrich, you have not the right to leave the decision of this question to the council. The matter is already decided; the Spirit of God [through the Bible] decides it."

Ask God to give you courage to do what is right at any cost.

Fourth Day. Pray in Jesus' Name.

Read John 15:6, 13, 14; 1 Timothy 2:5.

We pray to God through Jesus Christ. It is useless to pray to Mary or the apostles. They were mere human beings. They cannot forgive our sins nor save us. To pray in Jesus' name is not to use his name as some magic button which we press to get results. To pray in his name means that we love him and live for him. As the Bible says, we "remain in him." Only then can we ask what we will, and expect it to be given to us. John 15:7. Look up the word "mediator" in the dictionary. Read 2 Timothy 2:5 again with this meaning in mind.

Thank Jesus for his death on the cross, making it possible for you to speak to God.

Fifth Day. We are Saved by Faith.

Read Ephesians 2:1-10.

Martin Luther, like Menno Simons, was an unhappy Catholic priest. He was restless because he did not have peace with God. He still had his sins. He tried everything he could to get rid of his sin. He fasted and prayed. He abused himself by doing such things as sleeping in a cold room without cover. He went on a long journey to Rome to see the relics of the saints and to climb a sacred stairs which he was told was Pilate's stairs. No matter what he did, he knew that he was still a sinner and could not be good enough to please God.

Then one day he read Romans 1:17: "the righteous will live by faith." Suddenly he realized that sinners are not saved by *trying* but rather by *trusting*. He received Jesus Christ as Savior, his sins were forgiven, and the peace of God flooded his soul.

Trust in Christ for your salvation, and thank him for the peace he gives.

Sixth Day. The Christian Life Is the Holy Life.

Read 1 Thessalonians 5:14-22.

The early Mennonites insisted from the start that their new faith must bear fruit in pure living. Conrad Grebel told an early applicant for baptism that to be a member of the church one must be free from adultery, gambling, drunkenness, and other evil practices of the day.

Kessler described the daily life of the Mennonites as follows: "Their daily walk and behavior seems to be upright, godly, and entirely blameless. They do not wear expensive clothing and do not eat or drink too much. Their clothing is simple, and they wear broad felt hats. They go about humbly, and do not carry weapons. They seem much more concerned about right living than do the Catholics."

How important is it to live a holy life? Hebrews 12:14.

Ask God to help you live a holy life.

Seventh Day. The Christian Life Is the Way of Love.

Read Romans 12:17-21.

Dirk Willems, a Dutch Mennonite, was fleeing for his life. As he ran, he came to a canal which was partly frozen over. He would be risking his life to cross on the thin ice. To stay meant arrest and possible death. He decided to go on, and crossed the canal. His pursuer was not so fortunate and fell through the ice.

Here was Willems' opportunity to escape. But instead he returned and rescued his enemy. His enemy would have released him had it not been for an officer standing on the bank who de-

Dirk Willems, a Dutch Mennonite, saves his captor's life, 1569. Willems was later burned at the stake.

manded his arrest. Willems was later burned at the stake. This is how a Christian should treat his enemies. Such love comes only from above.

Ask God to fill your heart with the love of Christ.

Working for Jesus

1. Give tracts to people you meet.
2. Visit a sick person.
3. Pray for missionaries and Christians in other countries.
4. Ask your parents whether you can help them with their work. Always respond gladly when they ask you to help.
5. Buy a Testament and give it to someone who does not have one.
6. Read a Bible story to your younger brother or sister or to some other child.
7. Prepare a scrapbook to give to a shut-in friend.
8. Tell an unsaved person about Jesus.
9. Take an unsaved person your age along to church with you.
10. Pray for that unsaved person.
11. Organize a Bible Story Hour for the small children of your neighborhood one evening a week for one-half hour, say from 4:30 to 5:00 p.m.
12. Pray for a person who may have mistreated you.
13. Save part of your earnings or allowance and put it into the offering.
14. Watch for an opportunity to help your minister with some work—lawn-mowing, or whatever.
15. Build up a prayer list.
16. Write a letter to some old person.
17. Write a letter to a church worker in another state, province, or country.
18. Ask God for help in overcoming a sin in your life.

Memory Verses

These verses may also be memorized from such versions as the RSV or Today's English Version. Free translations and paraphrases such as *The Living Bible* are not recommended for memorization.

God is spirit, and his worshipers must worship in spirit and in truth. John 4:24.

Everyone who sins breaks the law; in fact, sin is lawlessness. 1 John 3:4.

Just as Moses lifted up the snake in the desert, so the Son of Man must be lifted up, that everyone who believes in him may have eternal life. For God so loved the world that he gave his one and only Son, that whoever believes in him shall not perish but have eternal life. John 3:14-16.

That if you confess with your mouth, "Jesus is Lord," and believe in your heart that God raised him from the dead, you will be saved. For it is with your heart that you believe and are justified, and it is with your mouth that you confess and are saved. Romans 10:9, 10.

Therefore, if anyone is in Christ, he is a new creation; the old has gone, the new has come! 2 Corinthians 5:17.

I write these things to you who believe in the name of the Son of God so that you may know that you have eternal life. 1 John 5:13.

Those who accepted his message were baptized, and about three thousand were added to their number that day. They devoted themselves to the apostles' teaching and to the fellowship, to the breaking of bread and to prayer. Acts 2:41, 42.

But grow in the grace and knowledge of our Lord and Savior Jesus Christ. To him be glory both now and forever! Amen. 2 Peter 3:18.

No temptation has seized you except what is common to man. And God is faithful; he will not let you be tempted beyond what you can bear. But when you are tempted, he will also provide a way out so that you can stand up under it. 1 Corinthians 10:13.

Then he said to them all: "If anyone would come after me, he must deny himself and take up his cross daily and follow me." Luke 9:23.

But his delight is in the law of the Lord, and on his law he meditates day and night. Psalm 1:2.

The boundary lines have fallen for me in pleasant places; surely I have a delightful inheritance. Psalm 16:6.